A Brief History

ST. ANDREW'S
SHRIVENHAM

*'Is not time even as love is,
undivided and paceless?'*

Kahlil Gibran, *The Prophet*

A BRIEF HISTORY

OF

END-TIME

Paula Clifford

A LION BOOK

Copyright © 1997 Paula Clifford
This edition copyright © 1997 Lion Publishing

The author asserts the moral right
to be identified as the author of this work

Published by
Lion Publishing plc
Sandy Lane West, Oxford, England
ISBN 0 7459 3460 9

First edition 1997
10 9 8 7 6 5 4 3 2 1 0

Acknowledgments
Biblical quotations are from
The Revised Standard Version of the Bible
© 1952 and 1971

A catalogue record for this book is available
from the British Library

Typeset in 11/12 Lapidary 333
Printed and bound in Great Britain by
Caledonian International Book Manufacturing, Glasgow

Contents

Acknowledgments

Anyone who works in Oxford has reason to be grateful for the facilities offered by its university libraries. I would like to thank particularly the staff of the Bodleian Library and the Librarian of Magdalen College for their unfailing helpfulness when I have been seeking out somewhat obscure publications. My thanks, too, to Malcolm Deboo of Zoroastrian House in London and to the children and teachers of Eaton Park Primary School in Stoke-on-Trent and the St John Fisher Roman Catholic High School in Newcastle-under-Lyme for their special contributions to this book. Finally I would like to thank my own children – Richard, Joanna and Tim – who have each helped and supported me in their different ways, together with many friends and colleagues who have stimulated my thinking and listened patiently to my ideas.

Where's It All Going to End?

'Eternity's a terrible thought. I mean, where's it all going to end?'

Tom Stoppard,
Rosencrantz and Guildenstern are Dead

What's so special about the year 2000? The logical answer would be 'not a lot'. To start with, the reckoning of 2,000 years of modern time is not strictly accurate. The estimate of the date of the birth of Christ, from which we measure the years 'AD', was done in the sixth century and was about six years out, not to mention the ten days or so that were 'lost' when the calendar was adjusted in the sixteenth century. Then, of course, there are the Muslim countries who do things differently anyway, calculating their calendar as beginning in AD622, the year of Muhammad's flight from Mecca.

But logic is not a particularly important consideration when it comes to looking at the power of numbers. Indeed almost any date can be made to seem extraordinarily significant if it is given enough hype. There was, for example, the mystique that surrounded 1984 – the title of George Orwell's novel written thirty-five years before, which predicted the arrival of Big Brother, the Thought Police and the rewriting of history. We surely breathed a collective sigh of relief as the year came and went, no better and no worse than any other in its decade.

The passing of a millennium does, though, seem to be a particular focus for all kinds of hopes and fears. For Westerners the number is deeply rooted in Christian tradition, ever since the writer of Revelation had a vision of

Satan being bound for 1,000 years, and it is closely associated with predictions about the end of the world as we know it. But the question 'where will it all end?' is not, as we shall see, the sole province of millennialists, those people whose faith hinges on the idea of world-changing events taking place at the end of 1,000 years – quite the opposite. Questions about when, how and why our world will end seem to have been asked by all kinds of people down the ages since recorded history began, and they will probably continue to exert a fascination in the third millennium as well.

The signs of people's obsession with such questions in the past remain around us for all to see here and now, and in this book I want to use them as a basis for a series of personal investigations into the future as it has been represented in the past as well as in the present. Along the way I will be looking for answers to a variety of questions: How did our ancestors envisage and look forward to the end of time? Are our ideas at the end of the twentieth century any different? Where will it all end? Does it matter?

It takes no more than a short imaginative leap in time, back about 100 years to the streets of London in the closing years of the nineteenth century to find an example of what I have in mind. This is the kind of scene beloved of the old black and white film-makers who set their tales of suspense amid the capital's gas lamps and swirling fog. The time is important. Queen Victoria, who came to the British throne as a girl of eighteen, is by now an old woman and there's a very real feeling that the end of an era cannot be far off. What's more, the 1890s have brought to literary and artistic circles a general atmosphere of decadence and a mood of despondency, both of which have, historically, often accompanied the transition from one age to the next. It has been dubbed *fin de siècle* – a sort of end-of-century blues.

Now imagine that onto this London scene there enters the awkward figure of a sandwich-board man. The wooden boards at the front and back of his body, which hamper the natural movements of his limbs, proclaim a dismal message: 'Repent, for the end of the world is nigh. Prepare to meet thy doom.' This is a member of the Christadelphian sect founded some fifty years earlier in America. These 'brothers of Christ' believe that Jesus will soon return and rule the world from Jerusalem for 1,000 years. They have scoured the Bible for prophecies they can apply to their own time, and their message offers little comfort to the fashionable crowds of the 1890s, even if they are disposed to listen to it.

So let's leave the unsmiling Christadelphian to walk the city streets and look for more entertaining things. A nearby concert hall is advertising the performance of a new work by the young Bavarian composer Richard Strauss. *Thus Spake Zarathustra* is an orchestral tone poem with a long subtitle: 'Symphonic optimism in *fin de siècle* form, dedicated to the twentieth century'; certainly the composer's use of the twelve-tone scale will sound somewhat futuristic to the ears of the average concert-goer and may well inspire not so much optimism as perplexity. The new piece is a musical description of nature and the rise of humankind from primitive being to 'superman', represented by Zarathustra. Zarathustra is a key figure. He is more commonly known as Zoroaster, an Iranian prophet who may have lived as early as the fifteenth century BC and whose philosophy was well established in the Babylonian empire of the sixth century BC. According to Zoroaster the world is a battlefield on which forces of good and evil confront each other, although the odds are slightly weighted in favour of good, and his writings stress the idea that one day the world will return to the happy state in which it began. Is it coincidence that a musical work composed in a decade when people were getting increasingly restless and were looking forward, however apprehensively, to the beginning of a new century and a new era, should bring with it echoes of ancient aspirations to something very similar? As we shall see, Zoroastrianism is the earliest of today's religions to contain a sense of the present world order coming to an end. And the pattern that it suggests, of tensions and conflict heralding the last days, is one that strikingly recurs throughout history irrespective of differences of time, place and culture.

Back on the streets of Victorian London, a visit to the nearest bookshop offers further variations on the same theme. A recent best-seller is a short story by the young writer H.G. Wells called *The Time Machine*. This little book revolutionized English literature on its first appearance in 1895 with what Wells' biographer would later call 'a masterful marriage of the fictive art and theoretical science'. The time traveller of Wells' story journeys first thousands, then millions of years into the future. There he finds that human beings have divided into two species: tiny mindless innocents who live above the ground and their evil subterranean counterparts, until both groups are replaced by giant creepy crawlies. The sun gets bigger and redder, the moon disappears, the stars slow down and eventually the earth comes to rest with one face turned to the sun. As life ebbs away from the earth the time traveller watches –

'with a strange fascination the sun grow larger and duller in the westward sky... At last, more than thirty million years hence, the huge red-hot dome of the sun had come to obscure nearly a tenth part of the darkling heavens.'

Is this where it will all end? And does anyone really care? Certainly the end of the world is the stuff of science fiction, but is it of serious concern to anyone other than a handful of religious fanatics? Well, if we take these few examples from different areas of life in a bygone age as typical of their time, it seems as though lots of people cared, at least then, at least sometimes. But what about now? Is it even conceivable that sophisticated Westerners of the 1990s should have anything at all in common with the spirit of their Victorian ancestors a century before?

If we update our imaginary London scene, the gas lamps and the fog (a product of Victorian industrialization) have of course disappeared, along with the social and artistic malaise peculiar to that century's end. But there can be no doubt that they have been succeeded by new concerns. Take the fog, for example. As the harmful effects on our planet of successive ages of industrialization have become more apparent, environmentalists have generated a new wave of unease, causing us to wonder just how long the earth can go on supporting human life. The swirling fog – a cliché of fear for novelists and film-makers alike – has become an even more chilling symbol of the unwitting damage inflicted on the earth over the past century.

Perhaps the most significant contribution of the twentieth century to world history will prove to be its recognition of the potentially devastating effect that humankind has had on the planet earth. The consequences of industrialization and later technology on human beings themselves are horrific enough, with new links being discovered almost daily between working conditions and life-threatening cancers and other illnesses. And to these must be added such disasters as the Chernobyl nuclear reactor explosion in 1986, making an area of Russia uninhabitable for the foreseeable future, the insidious processes of pollution and deforestation, especially in developing countries, and the effect of industrial products such as CFCs, not just on the air we breathe but also on the vital unseen areas above the earth's atmosphere.

Is it already too late to halt this progression towards ecological disaster? Ecologists have borrowed the language of religious prophets, ancient and modern, in speaking of the damage already done and the bleak outlook for the future. Like the Garden of Eden, wrote the ecologist Jonathon Porritt, 'the earth has been marred by human folly'. The gloomy predictions of the environmentalists are uncannily reminiscent of the millennialists' forecasts of disasters to come, but with the crucial difference that it remains within the power of human beings to save themselves and their world. Our fate is seen not so much as God's judgment and retribution but as one of our own making.

But the new eco-prophets of doom have not completely taken over from religious groups in proclaiming the imminent end of the world as we know it. The ancient prophecies of Zoroaster had a profound influence on other religions, affecting Jewish ideas about the end of the present age which then in turn influenced the development of Christian thought.

The Christadelphian sandwich-board man can still be seen patrolling London's Oxford Street, and I clearly remember the strange mixture of fear and embarrassment whenever I encountered his double in the seaside town where I grew up. But whereas his version of Christianity may once have been a fairly rare departure from orthodox belief, the late twentieth century has seen a huge proliferation of sects of all kinds, some with their roots in Christianity or other world religions, but many more founded on some form of nature religion. Many of them exist primarily because of a belief in the imminent end of the world and may only come to public attention when something goes horribly wrong. In 1994 an obscure 'doomsday' sect, the Order of the Solar Temple, leapt into the international news when dozens of its members apparently committed mass suicide in two separate parts of Switzerland, along with some deaths in Canada. Commentators were quick to draw parallels with other horrific events: the mass suicide of 914 people in Guyana in 1978 and the death of David Koresh and eighty-two of his followers in Waco, Texas, fifteen years later.

Far from being an outmoded concern, interest in the end of the world runs amazingly high, and inevitably this is reflected in different aspects of our culture. Even my Victorian examples are still going strong. *The Time Machine* is that rare phenomenon, a book which has never gone out of print; and the opening bars of Strauss' *Zarathustra* provided Stanley Kubrick with unforgettable music to the film *2001 – A Space Odyssey*.

Nowadays, though, it is not necessary to look to fiction, or science fiction, for ideas about the earth's future. As astronomers and cosmologists have refined their theories about the origin of the universe, so too they have been able to theorize about its end. They can even put some kind of date on it; but the timescale involved in the process whereby the universe might cease to expand and begin to collapse in on itself is so great that it can hardly cause us any serious unease. Long before the billions, if not trillions, of years that remain for our universe have elapsed, there seems a fair chance that the human race will have destroyed itself or its planet.

But for many people this may seem too rational. It is strange but true that while the twentieth century has seen extraordinary progress in human knowledge about ourselves, the earth and the universe, together with developments in technology that non-specialists can barely begin to get their brains round, at the same time interest in prophecies and soothsaying seems never to have been stronger. One example will do for now.

Each autumn there appears an almanac of predictions for the year ahead based on the writings of a rather obscure doctor-cum-astrologer, who lived in Provence some 450 years ago. Nostradamus' 'prophéties' were eagerly discussed at the French court of his day, and were probably written for it. But their wording, when it is comprehensible, is often so general that commentators have had a field day applying them to world events up to the present day. Nostradamus' reference to 'a kingdom in dispute divided between brothers' has been seen by one American commentator (who seems none too strong on historical detail) as predicting the abdication of Edward VIII and the accession of George VI. It's easy enough to apply such sayings in retrospect, but quite another matter to use them as a day-by-day guide to the year ahead. Even so, sales of the almanac both in France and England, and no doubt elsewhere, seem as good as ever.

Nostradamus may have had more to say about the collapse of empires than about the end of the world, but calculations as to when this might happen appear with surprising regularity. Such predictions have a long pedigree. The Old Testament book of Daniel, probably written in the second century BC, predicts the end in 'seventy weeks of years', which is usually interpreted as seventy multiplied by seven (the number of days in a week), i.e. 490 years hence. By the nineteenth century some biblical scholars, with a spectacular disregard for scientific investigation even then, had decided that the world was created in 4004BC and would end in AD1911.

This book is a personal exploration of our collective fascination with why, when and how our world will end. It will involve a journey through history which will take us from Zoroastrianism to Latin literature, from Jewish to Christian prophecies down the centuries, and across the continents from

Europe to the United States. Along the way we shall encounter prophets and charlatans, scientists and astrologers, people with deep religious convictions and those with none, as well as times of national disaster – such as the Black Death in England – when people's thoughts turned to the end-times.

Art, literature and folklore all have their place here, for perhaps more than anything else they are indicators of the extent of people's interest in the 'end things'. This interest, not to say obsession, is reflected in ancient paintings on medieval church walls depicting the horrors of the last judgment. It's there too in the work of a twelfth-century French poet who described vividly the 'signs' of the end: when the dead will be borne away on tremendous winds and the rainbow will fall from the sky. A few centuries later, a Yorkshire soothsayer, Mother Shipton of Knaresborough, also recounted the signs of the end in rhyme, though in a style which is more akin to doggerel than great verse:

> The time shall come when seas of blood
> Shall mingle with a greater flood.

What is the point of this journey through time? Although the advent of the year 2000 does not mean that it is exactly 2,000 years since the birth of Christ, the power of the number – the end of the second millennium, give or take a bit – is such that it automatically brings with it a rash of questions about when it will all end. The point of this brief history therefore has to be not just to look and learn but also to evaluate: to try to see what 'the end of the world' has meant for people in the past, how far these meanings are part of our present heritage, and what pointers they may give us for the future.

Note: I have done my best to avoid specialist jargon, but there are two terms which will inevitably crop up. One is 'eschatology', which has to do with 'the last things'; the other is 'apocalyptic', which literally means revealing what is hidden. As we shall see, though, the word apocalpytic has come to be used of any dramatic representation of the last things, and (particularly in popular usage) of any event that may precipitate the end, as well as designating a particular type of literature whose subject-matter relates to events at the end of time.

Chapter 1

The Beginning
of the End

*'By the early Neanderthal period it is a virtual certainty
that humankind already anticipated some kind of afterlife.'*

Robert Heilbroner, *Visions of the Future: The Distant Past,
Yesterday, Today, Tomorrow*

The child's question 'Where did I come from?' is not necessarily the demand for a sex lesson at the tender age of five or six that adults usually take it to be. Children are well aware that there was a time when they did not exist, and for them it was only a short while ago. It is only natural to long to know what it was like before, and how this momentous change, from a state of 'not being' to their present state of being alive, took place. Gradually, though, as we grow up, away from that moment of coming into being, we lose that acute sense of the time when we 'were not'. So the question gets answered not by an appeal to the philosophical notion of consciousness but by biology and the simple 'facts' of life. And as the years pass, a new question takes its place: 'Where am I going? Is death really going to be the end of me?'

The more I have reflected on people's ideas on the end of the world, the more I am drawn to the conclusion that the child's instinctive question has its counterpart in our collective human consciousness. We sense there is significance for us in where the world came from and where it is going. These questions of the beginning and the end are often seen as inseparable and this has been the case for centuries. In the past Christians have sometimes taken their cue from the words of Jesus recorded in Matthew's gospel: 'As were the days of Noah, so will be the coming of the Son of man'

(Matthew 24:37). So in the seventeenth century the Flood – which in Genesis comes not so long after creation – was believed to have taken place in the year 1656BC. A neat balance would have been for the world to end in AD1656 and for a while this was a popular choice of date for the end. As for beginnings, the cosmologists tell us that our universe could be up to 15,000 million years old. That may seem a lot but it's not. It could last for many billions of years yet. And even though the human race has evolved in the last minute before midnight if we imagine the time from the origins of the universe to the present day as a 24-hour day, we are still, relatively speaking, very close to the beginning – close to the world's birth. But this is, of course, a relatively new concept. Back in the third century Hippolytus believed that when Christ was born the world was already old – 5,500 years old to be precise – and that it had only another 500 years to go.

Today plenty of people besides professional cosmologists would dearly love to know where the world came from, but still the question that is more commonly asked is about where the world is going. When, how, why will it end? What then? These questions have been around for a very long time and have occurred and recurred in many different guises. Possibly, as Heilbroner suggests, it all goes back to the Neanderthals who were alive 100,000 years ago (or at least to their distant cousins); he may also be right in believing that we ask such questions in order to cope with the finality of death. Certainly people down the ages have regularly anticipated the end of the world. And not only have their ideas been remarkably similar; they have also shared an astounding arrogance. Not only will the world end, but time and time again individuals, movements and religions have claimed special knowledge for themselves, insisting that they alone know when and how this will take place and what will happen afterwards. Undeterred by obvious failure when the promised time comes and goes, prophets continue to claim to know exactly when and how these things will come about.

The consciousness of the end of the world cannot be dismissed as a product of medieval religion or superstition. If that were the case, sophisticated postmodernist Westerners standing on the threshold of the third millennium would surely be immune to it, and there is abundant evidence to prove that we are not. Indeed if there is one thing that emerges with any certainty from all that is said and written about the end of the world, it is that speculation about it will continue as long as the human race survives.

So where did it all come from? I began the first of my investigations by looking for the oldest case of belief in the end of the world being incorporated into a religious system, and found it in Zoroastrianism, which turned out to be surprisingly close to home.

Zarathustra's legacy

The world's oldest revealed religion has its European headquarters in a north-west London suburb. The Zoroastrian Association of Europe was first established in England in 1861, not because of the attractions of the capital but because Zoroastrians were looking for somewhere to bury their dead. This they found in 1863 near Guildford in Surrey, where the country's first non-denominational cemetery had been established at Brookwood.

At the Zoroastrians' West Hampstead headquarters I was given a careful explanation of this choice of cemetery. To a Zoroastrian death represents the triumph of evil, albeit a temporary one. To bury the dead in the ground is to defile the earth which is not evil, but which is counted as one of God's creations. Cremation, though, is worse, because it involves fire which is particularly revered in Zoroastrianism as the living symbol of truth. Traditionally in the East – the home of Zoroastrianism – the ecologically minded believers would leave corpses unburied, so that vultures could clean away decaying flesh from the bones. But in a Western country with no vultures and a culture in which the idea of leaving the dead undisposed of was abhorrent, the Brookwood cemetery was a compromise. Here the Zoroastrians could take over a plot of land and make of it a garden. The Hanging Gardens of Babylon, I was informed, were after all a Zoroastrian idea, and here in suburban Surrey the evil of death would in some way be offset by the symbolic reminder of deserts being made green, of good overcoming evil.

It is only recently that people have begun to take note of the importance of Zoroastrianism in the development of Judaism and Christianity, particularly in respect of the evolution of ideas about events at the end of time. Yet whereas Judaism and Christianity have their historical documents and their holy scriptures, the Zoroastrians' knowledge of their religious origins is much less clear-cut. Because their tradition has always been a predominantly oral one, even the most basic details have come down in a variety of forms and are open to widely differing interpretations. There are, for example, three dates associated with the coming of the religion's founder, the prophet Zarathustra (this is his Iranian name; Zoroaster is the

Western variant). Two of the dates come from within the Zoroastrian tradition itself: 600BC and 6000BC, both of them with symbolic overtones. The third date is 1500BC and this is the one most widely accepted nowadays, because it has a basis in linguistic evidence. On this showing, the religious ideas of Zarathustra were being formulated at roughly the time of Abraham, or perhaps a little later; and they predate the classical prophets of Judaism such as Amos and Hosea by at least 600 years.

It is likely, then, that the prophet was born into a semi-nomadic, pastoral people of the Early Iron Age. Where this community lived is as difficult to pinpoint as the date of Zarathustra's birth, although it is generally agreed that, having migrated from the Steppes of Central Asia, they eventually settled in eastern Iran, either in present-day Kazakhstan or Western Afghanistan. A notable high point of Zoroastrianism came in the sixth century BC when it became the official religion of the first Persian empire under Cyrus the Great in 549. It was at this time that the Jewish people, who had been captives in exile in Babylon for over fifty years, had their closest contact with Zoroastrian beliefs. The influence of these beliefs, together with Babylonian culture in general, permeated exilic and post-exilic Judaism and is reflected in its prophetic books, most notably chapters 40 to 66 of the Old Testament book of Isaiah. Zoroastrianism remained Iran's state religion until the seventh century AD, when the empire was attacked by Muslim armies and most Zoroastrians fled to India – which today is one of their major religious centres.

The only contemporary written source for Zarathustra's teaching consists of his own poems known as the *Gathas*, and even these do not exist in any modern edition. There are five poems, said to have been revealed to Zarathustra, and today these are the only teachings accepted by Zoroastrian fundamentalists. Although the oral tradition is partly responsible for the absence of other written texts, the major factor has been persecution. In the Middle Ages there were twenty-one volumes of the *Avesta* (the name of the ancient language of Zarathustra's revelation) made up of seven books on religion (including the *Gathas*), seven on law and seven on medicine. This intermingling of disciplines reflects the idea that Zoroastrianism is a whole way of life. The number of volumes is symbolic: it reflects the twenty-one words of the Zoroastrians' most sacred prayer. Today only one volume remains; the books were revised in the early Middle Ages and subsequently destroyed in the course of Islamic persecution of Zoroastrians in Iran.

Nonetheless Zoroastrianism has survived, as perpetual flames burning in temples across the world testify. It is only a small community; there are 7,000 believers in Europe, 5,000 of whom are based in London. The majority of its adherents – upwards of 120,000 – are in India and Iran, with a further 10,000 in North America. Despite its size it has its share of fringe fundamentalists and non-orthodox sects. The fringe includes those who, like their Jewish and Christian counterparts, take symbolic numbers to be literal and try to calculate the exact date on which the world will end, the difference being that they have been at it for rather longer. But the Zoroastrian flames symbolize the persistence of a belief about the nature of the world, and in particular about its end, that was known to our distant ancestors who stood on the threshold of the Iron Age. What, then, do orthodox Zoroastrians believe and what are the echoes of that belief – echoes that have far outstripped the immediate confines of their ancient faith?

In a few hours one weekday evening the Librarian at the Zoroastrian headquarters, Malcolm Deboo, gave me a fascinating, and highly intensive introduction to the basic tenets of his faith. Quite rightly he insisted that I should know something about Zoroastrianism as a whole before focusing on one particular aspect of it. Three main factors emerged that for me were especially significant: the belief in a God who is wholly good, although not yet all powerful; the belief that the present world will end; and the belief that human beings have some control over when it will end.

Ahura Mazda

In the beginning, there were two Primal Spirits,
    Twins spontaneously active;
These are the Good and the Evil, in thought, and word, and in deed:
Between these two, let the wise choose aright;
Be good, not base.
(*The Divine Songs of Zarathustra*)

Fundamental to Zoroastrian belief is the clash between good and evil, though Malcolm was emphatic that I should not think of his religion in terms of dualism – good and evil as two aspects of divine power. For the Zoroastrian good is part of God and evil is not; indeed the divine force –

Ahura Mazda ('the Wise Lord' or 'Lord of Wisdom') – is made up of everything and anything that is good. Evil does not come from God but is the state of moving away from him. So far so good – not so very different from the idea of God as revealed in Genesis and espoused by Jews and Christians alike. But Zoroastrians differ fundamentally in their belief as to *why* the world was created at all. Before creation Ahura Mazda existed in a spiritual world of endless light, spoiled only by the existence of a little dark, that is, evil. From his perspective of total wisdom Mazda created the physical world in order to tempt evil out of its spiritual existence. Evil could then be trapped in the physical creations (there are seven of them – sky, water, earth, plants, cattle, man and fire) and the finest creation of all – man – would eventually destroy the force of evil. Unlike followers of later beliefs in a lost paradise on earth, Zoroastrians look forward to a paradise that in a sense has yet to be created – the spiritual and material worlds free from evil, a state of total goodness and harmony which they call the 'making wonderful'.

The Zoroastrian 'creed' is simple: 'good thoughts, good words, good deeds' – a sound enough principle to live by, but one with a deep spiritual aim: the total destruction of evil. The religion is unrelentingly optimistic. Malcolm explained that if evil is destroyed by individual good actions it is finally defeated when goodness reaches such a point that evil can no longer exist. As evil decreases it becomes more concentrated, so the disasters and upheavals of today's world which are generally viewed with gloom become for Zoroastrians a cause for hope. The upsurge in crimes of violence, for instance, is a sign of that concentrated evil which is even now being ground down by good.

The end of time represents the end of a process in the nature of Ahura Mazda himself, who is believed to be constantly evolving. Although very powerful, Mazda is not all-powerful, because he is unable to overcome the force of evil on his own (this is how suffering is explained – Mazda is said to be 'relatively non-omnipotent'). His power lies in his wisdom, but he will only become truly all-knowing and all-powerful when evil has been overcome at the end of time.

It has to be said that even within the Zoroastrian optimistic scheme of things, if the end of the world comes with the triumph of good, then it is still a very long way off indeed. The reason for this is human beings' free will. Given the freedom to choose between good deeds and bad, humans opt as much for the bad as for the good, though the Zoroastrians have no doctrine of original sin – they believe we are not inherently sinful. Our individual destiny after death will depend on the predominance of one or the other in our lives: in the words of one of the *Gathas* there will be 'long punishment for the evil-doer and bliss for the follower of Truth'.

Death and the end of time

Although widely understood by Zoroastrians as the temporary triumph of evil, death is the subject of some debate within the religion. Traditionally in the texts death was seen as a work of evil, which put a halt to goodness, but the influence of European culture has meant that some no longer see death as evil in itself. Beliefs as to what happens when we die are also somewhat vague, but Zoroastrianism has three elements that link it crucially with later religions: the idea of something happening three days after death, the concept of individual judgment of souls and the fate awaiting them of either heaven or hell, and the transformation of the earth itself in the events of the end.

After three days the soul is detached from its body and passes into the afterlife where it is to be judged. First, though, it must cross the 'Bridge of the Separator'. For the soul blessed with good thoughts, words and deeds, the bridge broadens out and it passes into a heaven – graded according to different levels of goodness. But for the wicked soul the bridge narrows until it becomes razor sharp and the soul is dragged down into a hell, not of fire, but a place which is cold, damp and smelly, to stay there until the end of time.

> Verily, the Right of the truthful man shall vanquish at last the
> Wrong of the wicked.
> Standing at the Bridge of Judgment,
> The Evil Soul shall behold open the path of the righteous;
> He strives to reach it, but his own deeds prove to be his fetters;
> Trembling and moaning, he finds that he fails.

At the end of time itself, with the destruction of evil, comes the final judgment of all the souls, probably followed by the resurrection of the body which is reunited with the soul. At that point time ceases to be, although for the individual soul time has already effectively stopped at death. The final cleansing in which all trace of evil is removed, is effected by the eruption of molten lava from earth's mountains. This reflects a balance between the beginning and the end. The mountains of Iran were believed to have been thrown up by the forces of evil; at the end the mountains will be flattened as molten metal flows out of them, penetrating the furthest corners of heaven and hell, filling them with endless light. Professor Norman Cohn is the scholar who has been most responsible for demonstrating the importance of Zoroastrianism to later beliefs on the end of the world. He writes that at the Zoroastrian end of time there will be 'a state from which every imperfection will have been eliminated… an eternity when history will have ceased and nothing more can happen; a changeless realm, over which the supreme god will reign with an authority which will be unchallenged for evermore.'

When I questioned Malcolm about the doctrine of bodily resurrection he admitted disarmingly that this is 'a grey area', another matter of debate in the absence of any authoritative religious texts. At the end of the cleansing process, he said, 'we don't know what happens next'.

For a religion that has traditionally viewed death as evil, there is still a fair amount of interest in the dead. Zoroastrians do not believe in reincarnation (although there is a non-orthodox branch, influenced by Buddhism, which does). Nonetheless the departed souls are remembered for ten days in each year at the Fravardigan Festival; during this period it is believed that the spirits of the dead revisit the earth.

The timing of the end

Although much in Zoroastrianism is uncertain, there appear to be some very precise numbers involved when it comes to calculating the end of time. According to some sources, the world was created to last 9,000 years, while others say 12,000. This is then subdivided into three or four periods of 3,000 years each. According to the 12,000-year scheme, the first two periods mark stages in the battle between good and evil. Human beings are created after 6,000 years, only to be perverted by evil. But after 9,000 years the arrival of the prophet Zarathustra tips the balance, and after the final 3,000-year period in which we now live, good will eventually triumph.

Unfortunately, if this scheme of things is taken literally, it is upset by the most recent dating of the prophet's life to 1500BC, which suggests that the world should have ended 500 years ago, though at the time of the Persian empire the year we know as AD1500 may still have seemed a suitably remote date, if the 3,000 years are to be understood literally. The majority of Zoroastrians, though, now view the 3,000-year intervals as symbolic, and the Greek idea that three and nine are ideal numbers may have a part in this. The symbolism is echoed in the Zoroastrians' traditional garment, the Sudreh – a short-sleeved vest divided into nine parts. This represents either the 9,000 years up to the birth of the prophet, or alternatively the 9,000-year period in which every Zoroastrian lives. At the centre of the garment's V-neck there is an important symbolic part which has another 'perfect' number, the number seven: this is the gireban or 'pocket of good deeds'. The Sudreh itself is made of white cloth, since white represents purity of thought, which helps the mind towards 'good thoughts'.

Using precise numbers to express an undefined period of time or the concept of wholeness or perfection may seem strange to twentieth-century minds, particularly since our modern languages are very well equipped to express abstract concepts relating to vast expanses of time. Let's not forget, though, that we have similar turns of phrase. Maybe researchers in centuries to come will hit the same problem with the English expression 'not in a month of Sundays', meaning, of course, 'never'. Will they puzzle over whether this is linguistic shorthand for a real sum along the lines of 'there are four Sundays in each month, so a month of Sundays must be the length of a month – 30 or 31 days – multiplied by 4, say 120?' If this seems unlikely, it is no more than what many commentators have tried to do with symbolic numbers in the Old Testament Book of Daniel or the Book of Revelation in the New Testament. The use of precise numbers to express an abstract idea or a long, perhaps indefinite period, finds one of its first recorded forms in Zoroastrianism and no doubt dates back much further.

In spite of these great lengths of time, Zarathustra's poems have a certain urgency to them, as though his contemporaries have not long to make up their mind between good and evil. Soon after Zarathustra's death there is a further development in the appearance of Saoshyants. These are 'saviours' or 'helpers', who, although human, help to destroy evil at the end of time. In one tradition there is a Saoshyant who will raise the dead for fifty-seven years before the end of time and the 'making wonderful'. Gradually they become figures of the end days and in some texts there are only three of them known as 'sons of Zarathustra' who are born to virgins and appear at the end of time.

While the date of the end is unspecified except in very general terms, some of the features that emerge from Zoroastrian traditions and texts have parallels in Judaism and Christianity. Besides the number symbolism there are the key figures who appear before the end, and the idea of an increase of evil which points ultimately to the triumph of good. One sign of this evil is that human beings will become smaller and weaker as the end approaches. They revert to the eating habits of primeval man, rejecting meat in favour of plants and milk, until ten years before the coming of the Saoshyants they stop eating altogether, but do not die, as material living becomes somehow spiritualized.

Logically, in Zoroastrianism, the timing of the end is in our hands. If we were all to opt for goodness, evil could quickly be defeated and we could all move on to the state of perfect harmony. Despite this reassuring idea, though, I was surprised to learn that the Zoroastrians do not actively seek converts to their religion and that they seem unperturbed by their small numbers. Perhaps this is because, as Mary Boyce puts it, 'Zoroastrianism is almost as much a religion of this world as Judaism'. So when Zoroastrians eventually came into contact with Christian ascetics in Persia, who spurned all the good things of this world, conflict was bound to ensue.

I visited Brookwood a few weeks later, on a weekend when English Heritage, which is now responsible for its upkeep, was holding open days for members of the public, even though the cemetery is open every day during the hours of daylight. Nowadays it is not especially well known for its commemoration of the dead of many different faiths and of none. Two world wars have transformed it into an imposing military cemetery which honours British allies of many different nationalities. A friendly postman directed me to a side entrance closed by huge iron gates which, he assured me, were not to keep the public out but to stop deer coming in and eating the rhododendrons.

Beyond the whitewashed splendour of the military graves, and the homeliness of the graves of the local Christian faithful, the cemetery has its eastern section. Apart from a small area given over to the Turkish air force these are all civilian graves, their headstones displaying Arabic, Persian and Turkish scripts, sometimes with English alongside them. There is a huge mausoleum with an inscription over the doorway proclaiming the occupant's origin: 'I am Nowrosjee Nashirwanjee Wadia of the ancient Aryan race of Persia a citizen of the loyal town of Bombay who lies here peacefully under the far-off sky of wide-famed Britain.' The crescent of Islam is prominent on a number of graves, but most give little clue, at least to the uninitiated Westerner, as to the beliefs of the deceased.

In this most remote part of Brookwood the peace of the autumn day was constantly disturbed by mainline trains screeching past beyond the trees and the none-too-distant shooting from the Army's ranges at Bisley. It wasn't quite the image of evil overcome by good that I had been expecting, but it was an untroubled garden nonetheless, and here I found the traces of Zoroastrianism that I had come to look for. On one or two graves there were the remains of a candle or nightlight, a symbol of the sacred fire. Others had headstones which might have been found anywhere else in the country but for the occasional reference to Ahura Mazda. Certainly the poetry was typical of the genre:

> He suffered patiently and long
> His hope was bright, his path was strong
> The peace of Ahura filled his breast
> And in his arms he sank to rest.

The tombstone of one Ardeshir Dadabhoy Chothia (born Bombay 1883, died London 1921) refers to crossing the bridge, though with what I had come to recognize as a characteristic vagueness as to detail. The carving is either hurried, or the work of a non-English speaker:

> He too has crossed the bridge 'twixt life and death whate'er
> these be: and whither beyond, who knows – an [sic] be it so,
> the light of Mazda dawn upon his soul with love refulcent [sic]
> and immortal repose.

But here again there is a compromise between East and West: the tomb contains cremated remains. In death as in life Zoroastrians have drawn freely from the cultures around them, which is very much in line with the precept of their prophet: 'Let each man choose his creed, with that freedom of choice which each must have at great events.'

But what of the other ancient religions and civilizations? Virtually every subject I have ever studied has begun with a look back not to Iran but to ancient Greece or ancient Egypt. Had I missed something by starting my explorations with Zarathustra?

The Egyptian way of death

Unlike the Zoroastrians the Ancient Egyptians had no concept of their world coming to an end. On the face of it this may seem surprising, given that their preoccupation with death is still very much in evidence to us thousands of years later in museums of antiquities across the world. In a Cambridge lecture in 1935 Sir Alan Gardiner commented on the paradox of a perfect life-giving Egyptian climate which at the same time made it very difficult to get rid of the evidence of death. He summed it up like this:

> In no country of the earth is life more attractive, more desirable; yet in no other country is death so nakedly revealed. Little wonder that the Egyptians conceived a fanatical abhorrence of death, and devoted no small part of their wealth to devising means of defeating it.

For the Egyptians, death was as life: they buried their treasures in their tombs – you could indeed 'take it with you'. Gardiner tells us that their massive tombs were called 'castles of eternity' and were modelled on the houses of the living, even to the extent (in the case of some of the most ancient tombs) of having their own lavatories. Bodily needs of food and clothing were expected to be provided by the family of the deceased, who were often bound by a contract to do this. The prospect of what would happen when the food ran out – as it surely would – was too dreadful to contemplate.

Much of what we know about the Egyptians' view of death comes from the writing and pictures on the walls of their tombs. Some of the inscriptions are taken from 'guidebooks' which describe the regions through which the soul must pass on its way to the 'abode of the blessed'. Not all the souls got there. Even though the Egyptians had no real concept of an end-time, they had a fairly well developed concept of hell, and believed that hell fire awaited those who did not believe in the great god Osiris or who failed to make offerings to him. It has been suggested that this may well have influenced Western views of hell in the Middle Ages

In addition, the Egyptians could and did express the idea of the natural order being overturned in certain circumstances. These lines date from about the middle of the third millennium BC and belong to the collection of writings known as the 'Pyramid texts':

> The sky is overcast
> The stars are darkened,
> The celestial expanses quiver,
> The bones of the earth-gods tremble,
> The planets are stilled,
> For they have seen the King appearing in power.

The vision of cosmic upheaval is one we shall encounter often. Across great stretches of time, from the distant past to the here and now, and into the future of science fiction, we shall hear much of the heavens shaking and the planets stopped in their paths. These lines are certainly the oldest writings I came across and they belong in a collection of over 500 'Utterances'. This particular one takes the form of a story in which a dead king, against a background of natural chaos, arrives in heaven. Once there he goes hunting and eats the gods, so that he himself becomes all-powerful:

> The King has appeared again in the sky,
> He is crowned as Lord of the horizon;
> He has broken the backbones
> And has taken the hearts of the gods…
> The King's lifetime is eternity. (no. 274)

The Egyptian concern to be surrounded in death by the things of life was a vital part of their religious system. It was important that the dead person should be buried with all that was necessary for his or her continuing existence in the next life – tools for domestic use, jewellery and cosmetics, and above all food. On death a person's spirit or personality ('ka') was set free from the body, but was still dependent on it for food. This meant that life after death was dependent on how well your surviving relatives looked after you in performing the funerary rituals and providing for the body's material needs. In addition, the body had to be preserved as perfectly as possible so that its spirit could eat the food provided for it, and for the well-to-do, at least, this took the form of mummification. Most of the mummies that survive today have a curious sameness about them. This is probably because they were deliberately stylized, made to look like the god Osiris, in the hope that the dead body would magically imitate Osiris in coming back to life after death.

The life that awaited at least the upper classes after death was of an otherworldly Egypt ruled by Osiris, although there are also tales of the soul journeying across the sky and down into the underworld each day with the sun-god Re, or living forever among the stars. Egyptian kings or Pharoahs (the name means 'son of Re' or Ra) were believed to be semi-divine, with a human mother and a god as a father. After death they joined the ranks of the gods, a process described in many of the Pyramid texts. Lesser mortals were not so fortunate, at least at the time of the Old Kingdom (the third millennium BC). The most that an Egyptian peasant could hope for was an eternity tilling land in the Fields of Reeds, although some centuries later, when the monarchy had suffered a decline, the afterlife began to be seen in more democratic terms. The moral behaviour of the individual in this life came to play its part, so that everyone could aspire to eternity on their own merits. The wicked, on the other hand, were destined for the underworld and a second death, if not eternal torment.

The point has already been made that Egyptian beliefs seem to contain no concept of time ever coming to an end. Their religious system was based on their observation of the world around them: a cycle of birth and death (seen in the rising and setting of the sun each day) and of death and rebirth (as vegetation withered away in the heat, only to be revived with the coming of rain). Like Egyptian art, religion reflected the society's stability, particularly during the Old Kingdom. The life cycle was repetitive and permanent, and there seemed to be no sense of impending doom. Yet the language of some of the Utterances, like the one already quoted, cannot be overlooked. Cosmic disorder is particularly striking in those Pyramid texts which describe the king ascending into the heavens. In one such the king ascends in an earthquake:

The sky thunders, the earth quakes, Geb quivers… the earth is hacked up… I ascend to the sky, my wing-feathers are those of a great bird… (no. 509)

while another includes the line 'the hail-storm is burst apart for me' (no. 511).

Not only are the language and imagery in place for describing events associated with the end of time. There is at least one period in Egypt's ancient history, during the Sixth Dynasty (2500–2000BC), when the collapse of royal power, and social disorder and decay seem to provide the typical conditions in which one might expect a general preoccupation with the eventual end of all things. This is well illustrated in an unusual group of poems under the title 'Dispute with his Soul of One who is Tired of Life' in which the pessimistic and self-questioning writer discusses with his spirit the attraction of suicide. The second poem deals with the theme of present decay:

To whom do I speak today?
None remembers the past,
None at this moment does good to him that has done it…
To whom do I speak today?

27

The sin that smites the land
It has no end.

In the face of this, the third poem deals with the attractive option of death:

Death is before me today
As a well-trodden path
As when a man returns from the war to his house.

Death is before me today
As when a man longs to see his house again
After he has spent many years in captivity.

In the end, though, the spirit persuades the unhappy poet that the hardships that lie ahead if no tomb is prepared for them would be unbearable and that it would be better for them to continue their life together, to 'follow the glad day and forget care'.

The Roman view

'Following the glad day' is a sentiment I remember from my A-level Latin days. It is echoed in Horace's 'carpe diem' meaning 'enjoy the present moment', though not far behind lurks the idea 'while you can'. And this points to a crucial difference in attitude between the Egyptians, with their unchanging world still as it was at the moment of creation, and the Greeks and the Romans. With the classical world comes a concept which was to make its way into the eschatology of both Jews and Christians, and which still remains influential today: the idea that the world is not only changing but changing for the worse.

The Greek poet Hesiod wrote of four ages of man, each one being worth less than the last. He saw his own time as the age of iron, the last of the series which began with gold and continued down through silver and bronze. Other Classical writers, among them Tibellus, Ovid, Juvenal and Lucian, conveyed the same idea in different terms: the past was a golden age, the age of Saturn; the present is the age of Jupiter. None of them admits the possibility that their present misfortune might be remedied; rather they see themselves as being on an inevitable downward path from the good that once was.

Rather depending on the state of the empire at the time, Rome itself would see its mythical descent from Romulus and Remus as exactly that – a downward progression, and there is no room for optimism. 'Most mythological history,' writes Heilbroner, 'looks back to a never-to-be-equalled past and looks forward to the future with indifference at best.' There is a sense that once upon a time humankind had everything: for Plato it was the age of the gods, for the Jews it was the Garden of Eden. Nowhere, or so historians tell us, is there any hint that such a paradise will one day be regained. Rather, as Borchardt has suggested, there seems to have been a widespread belief, across many different cultures, that the world was slowly but inexorably wearing out. These are, of course, sweeping generalizations. The fact that the majority of people believe one thing does not prevent others from believing the opposite. Most people today do not seriously think that the world will end in the year 2000; but a few people do believe precisely that, and hold to that belief with deep conviction.

Although the great ancient civilizations of Egypt, Greece and Rome did not develop their sketchy beliefs in an end-time very fully, they have undoubtedly left their mark on ours – political events from the sixth to the first century BC saw to that. Once the Jews started to return home from the 530s BC with astronomical and astrological ideas from Babylonia, they remained exposed to Zoroastrian thought through their Persian rulers until that empire was in turn overthrown by Alexander the Great who then conquered Palestine in 333–32BC. Alexander's policy was to impose Greek organization, institutions and culture on the cities he took over. And although the Jews in Palestine revolted against Greek tyranny in the second century and achieved independence in 142BC, they were all too quickly conquered again, this time by the Roman Pompey in the first century BC.

About forty years before the birth of Christ the Latin poet Virgil wrote a poem which does now look forward to a new Golden Age which is to be Rome's glorious future. It is his fourth 'Eclogue', which may have been written to celebrate the marriage of Antony and Octavia; it looks forward to the birth of their future child, which symbolizes an end once and for all to civil war which had plagued the Roman empire. It has so much in common with the style of Old Testament prophecy that some have treated it as a prophecy of Christ's birth:

Ours is the crowning era foretold in prophecy:
Born of Time, a great new cycle of centuries

> Begins. Justice returns to earth, the Golden Age
> Returns, and its first-born comes down from heaven above.

The Golden Age is reflected in the animal world: 'the ox will have no fear of the lion... snakes will die, and so will fair-seeming poisonous plants'; and for the agricultural community the hard labour of farming will come to an end:

> The soil will need no harrowing, the vine no pruning-knife;
> And the tough ploughman may at last unyoke his oxen.

But the new age is not of this world: nature is unnaturally at the service of man:

> We shall stop treating wool with artificial dyes,
> For the ram himself in his pasture will change his fleece's
> colour.

And although creation is united in its praise of its future state ('the whole creation exults in the age to come'), there remains no clue as to how or where these events may come about.

In general, then, well before the birth of Christ, developing Jewish thought on the end-time had been exposed to a wealth of conflicting ideas. Along with optimistic hopes of a new age there was the opposite pessimistic view that the world was in decline. Jewish writers could add these to their stock of borrowed or inherited concepts of a Zoroastrian judgment and end-time, and possibly of an Egyptian hell as well, together with the language for expressing such ideas. In addition, there was the general mythological heritage of the whole of the Ancient Near East. This is seen particularly in the Mesopotamian oral and epic poetry, some of which dates back to the third millennium BC, and includes an Epic of Creation and a story of the Flood. The Epic of Creation tells of monsters rising out of the waters of primeval chaos and of the struggle between the forces of chaos and order, until the waters of chaos are contained and earth and sky are separated (as in Genesis 1:7). These details later find an echo in the Christian vision of the end in the book of Revelation, with the final battle in heaven (Revelation 12) and the emergence of the beast from the sea (Revelation 13).

When we add to that mix the political turmoil of the second century BC in Israel, it is not surprising to find that it is from that period that eschatology really develops and takes off in the form of first Jewish then Christian apocalyptic writing.

References

Frank L. Borchardt, *Doomsday Speculation as a Strategy of Persuasian: A Study of Apocalypticism as Rhetoric*, Edwin Mellen Press, Lampeter, 1990.

E.A. Wallis Budge, *The Egyptian Heaven and Hell (the Book of Am-Tuat)*, London, 1925.

Norman Cohn, *Cosmos, Chaos and the World to Come: The Ancient Roots of Apocalyptic Faith*, Yale University Press, 1993.

Stephanie Dalley (translator), *Myths from Mesopotamia*, Oxford University Press, 1989.

A. Rosalie David, *Ancient Egyptians: Religious Beliefs and Practices*, Routledge and Kegan Paul, 1982.

R.O. Faulkner, *The Ancient Egyptian Pyramid Texts*, Oxford University Press, 1969.

Alan H. Gardiner, *The Attitude of the Ancient Egyptians to Death and the Dead*, Cambridge University Press, 1935.

Robert Heilbroner, *Visions of the Future: The Distant Past, Yesterday, Today, Tomorrow*, Oxford University Press, 1995.

D.J. Irani, *The Divine Songs of Zarathustra (with introduction by Rabindranath Tagore)*, London, George Allen and Unwin Ltd, 1924.

Virgil, *The Eclogues* (translated by C. Day Lewis), Oxford University Press, 1966.

Chapter 2

Writing About the End

'The Jews borrowed copiously and, it may be argued, at times unwisely, from Zoroastrian beliefs and practices, especially in the field of eschatology and angelology.'

Abba Hillel Silver, *Where Judaism Differs*

The British Museum in London is home to the so-called Cyrus Cylinder. This records how Cyrus of Persia captured Babylon in 539BC and sent expatriate prisoners back to their own countries. I thought I ought to see it, since it seemed to be a tangible sign of Zoroastrian influence penetrating not only the religion of the Jews in exile in Babylon but through them later Judaism in Palestine.

The cylinder is a slender barrel-shaped piece of terracotta, only twenty-five centimetres long and covered with writing. To read it, you would simply rotate it gently. I assumed – wrongly – that I would find it in the room containing treasures of sixth-century Babylonia (what the Museum calls 'later Mesopotamia') but eventually came across it in the area given over to ancient Iran. I eavesdropped on a small group of visitors who were being lectured by a well-informed guide. According to the cylinder, we were told, Cyrus had conquered Babylon and found that the worship of the Babylonian god Marduk had been neglected by the Babylonian king Nabonidus. Cyrus claimed to have sent home the gods and peoples of many towns in Mesopotamia and south-west Iran. There is no specific mention of the Jews, but it is always assumed that they were included in this general religious policy of repatriation (although it is known that some chose to stay behind). The guide had her own bit of background material to add. According to the historian Herodotus, Cyrus' army diverted the Euphrates and entered Babylon with ease, because everyone was busy attending a religious festival.

I was intrigued to discover that the cylinder, although in remarkably good shape for a piece of terracotta more than 2,500 years old, was not as well preserved as some of the other cylinders in the museum. And for me these cylinders were more interesting. A number of them were Babylonian calendars: a table of eclipses observed in the early part of the fifth century BC; an astronomical diary for a year in the fourth century BC; and another one for the year 164 to 163BC, which included observations of Halley's comet for a week in late September 164BC. These calendars were a reminder of the great skills of the Babylonians in astronomy – diaries were kept to record daily observations from as far back as the seventh century BC. It is hardly far-fetched to suppose that well-educated Jews in exile absorbed some of this information as well, and we can assume that they took home with them an interest in the changing pattern of the night sky and in calendars (the subject-matter of the Book of Jubilees which is sometimes dated as early as the fifth century BC). Certainly it was only with the Babylonian experience that the style of Jewish writing known as 'apocalyptic' began to emerge clearly. And it is this we need to consider now, to uncover the most obvious roots of virtually all thinking about end-time in the Western world.

Prophetic voices

A friend of mine once remarked, with a certain flamboyant confidence that went with his new status as a recently ordained curate, that the Old Testament prophet Ezekiel was 'a bit of a nutter'. Certainly Ezekiel was something of a visionary, who is probably best remembered for his prophecy of dry bones coming alive; and his description of creatures with four faces and wheels with their rims full of eyes (Ezekiel 1) is more than a little bizarre. More to the point, though, is that Ezekiel was writing in Babylon, five years or so into the period of the Jewish exile. His main theme, which has to do with judgment, is one that is fairly typical of later apocalyptic style; and he expresses it in terms which both reflect some Babylonian influence and are characteristic of more extreme apocalyptic writing later on.

It does not seem to me very likely that this particular style of writing appeared in embryonic form with Ezekiel in the sixth century BC, only to re-emerge fully fledged some 400 years later. There are hints of it already in a couple of the pre-exilic prophets: the reference to the day of the Lord's judgment in Zephaniah 1:15 as 'a day of clouds and thick darkness' and as a time when 'the sun shall be turned to darkness and the moon to blood' in Joel 2:31. And I believe that the main elements of apocalyptic style were well known when Ezekiel was writing, not least because, as we have seen, some of the ideas had already been around in neighbouring cultures for a considerable time. But apocalyptic by itself is usually a style rather than a story. Details like signs of the end or the idea that the world is in an irreversible decline are generally there to support something else; in the Old Testament they may lend weight to a prophecy of God's judgment on the nations hostile to Israel, while in the Middle Ages they may form the spectacular backdrop to a secular account of the death of a hero. It seems that it is only when the outlook is particularly bleak, when people share a real conviction that the end must be just around the corner, that apocalyptic signs and events become the main point of writing, a story in their own right.

Ezekiel uses the style he knew, or perhaps borrowed from his Babylonian captors, in a very specific and personal way. Apart from chapter 1 (which I shall return to in chapter 3 because of its parallels with the New Testament book of Revelation) Ezekiel 38 and 39 use apocalyptic detail to enhance and underline a particular message. These two chapters are a prophecy of an attack on the people of Israel by Gog, ruler of Magog, which arouses God's anger. Israel is victorious and the people are able to return to their homeland.

This is how the prophet sees the arrival of Gog in Israel:

On that day there shall be a great shaking in the land of Israel; the fish of the sea, and the birds of the air, and the beasts of the field, and all creeping things that creep on the ground, and all the men that are upon the face of the earth, shall quake at my presence, and the mountains shall be thrown down, and the cliffs shall fall, and every wall shall tumble to the ground. I will summon every kind of terror against Gog, says the Lord God; every man's sword will be against his brother. With pestilence and bloodshed I will enter into judgment with him; and I will rain upon him and his hordes and the many peoples that are with him, torrential rains and hailstones, fire and brimstone (38:19-22).

The chaos and destruction in nature as well as in human affairs are typical elements of apocalyptic that are used and reused by Jewish and Christian writers alike for centuries to come. Here, though, they are not deployed for their own sake. Rather, they are expressions of God's anger (his 'blazing wrath', 38:19) and a sign of his greatness: 'So I will show my greatness and my holiness and make myself known in the eyes of many nations. Then they will know that I am the Lord' (38:23). Later on, the idea of God being behind these terrors to come ceases to be made explicit, if indeed it is present at all.

The theme of God's greatness continues into chapter 39 which introduces the idea of a sacrificial banquet. It is a grim picture: birds and beasts are summoned to feast off the remains of the defeated warriors of God. And again it has a particular purpose, which is to demonstrate God's power and judgment. There is a vision of the fulfilment of this prophecy in Revelation 19:18. The motif of birds and animals in general becomes a familiar one in this style of writing, and the so-called eschatological banquet is a theme which will be particularly developed by Christian writers.

A couple of centuries on from Ezekiel, in a late addition to a much earlier text, we find evidence of a peculiarly Jewish feature of apocalyptic writing. This is the belief that at the end of time God will reunite his people:

> In that day the Lord will... recover the remnant which is left of his people, from Assyria, from Egypt, from Pathros, from Ethiopia, from Elam, from Shinar, from Hamath, and from the coastlands of the sea. He will raise an ensign for the nations, and will assemble the outcasts of Israel, and gather the dispersed of Judah from the four corners of the earth (Isaiah 11:11-12).

An important detail here, incidentally, is that this gathering in is to be effected by God himself. As we shall see in due course, American intervention in the affairs of Israel in the twentieth century in a self-interested attempt to hasten the end by encouraging Jews to return to their homeland, looks suspiciously like trying to do God's work for him.

A major factor in the dispersion of the Jews was the exile in Babylon, since many people subsequently chose to remain there and they established a community which survived until the Middle Ages. But this breaking up of the nation had in fact begun several centuries earlier, when Assyrian conquerors had sent Jewish craftsmen to other parts of their empire. In addition, Jews had also gone as refugees to Egypt. The upshot of all this was that in the period following the exile the majority of the people were scattered across Mesopotamia and along the coasts of the eastern Mediterranean.

The references in the first part of Isaiah to this dispersion and the prophecy of an eventual return are known to be later additions dating from the third or fourth centuries BC. These additions are the verses from chapter 11 already quoted and the whole of chapters 24 to 27, a section which ends with a reference to the return and including the important detail of worship:

> In that day a great trumpet will be blown, and those who were lost in the land of Assyria and those who were driven out to the land of Egypt will come and worship the Lord on the holy mountain at Jerusalem (Isaiah 27:13).

Isaiah 24–27 deals with events at the end ('the day of the Lord'), promising not only universal judgment and punishment for the sinful, but also a new age, a time of rejoicing. Here the end-time itself has become the main subject-matter, and the idea of God's intervention to 'lay waste to the earth' is expanded in detail over thirteen verses in chapter 24, stressing its inescapable universality. The writer is a poet. He is not content just to restate familiar signs of the end, to record merely that 'the foundations of the earth tremble' (24:18). He goes on:

> The earth is utterly broken,
> the earth is rent asunder,
> the earth is violently shaken.
> The earth sways like a drunken man,
> it sways like a hut;
> its transgression lies heavy upon it,
> and it falls, and will not rise again (24:19-20).

No one on earth is exempt from God's punishment, nor are 'the host of heaven' (24:21), while the sun and moon are both darkened: 'Then the moon will be confounded and the sun ashamed' (24:23).

When the writer turns to describing the joys to come, he includes the notion of an eschatological banquet, 'the Lord of hosts will make for all peoples a feast of fat things' (25:6), at a time when death is 'swallowed up for ever', when 'the Lord God will wipe away tears from all faces' (25:8) and when the bodies of the dead will arise (26:19).

Despite the presence of a number of important details which are taken up and developed by later apocalyptic writers, Isaiah 24–27 lacks the oppressive intensity that seems to me to characterize much of the later writing. I think this is again due to the poetic nature of most of the passage. This poetic touch lightens the overall tone and clearly indicates that for those who fear God the Day of the Lord is not all bad:

> Thy dead shall live, their bodies shall rise.
> O dwellers in the dust, awake and sing for joy!
> For thy dew is a dew of light,
> and on the land of the shades thou wilt let it fall (26:19).

Waiting for the Messiah

One of the most distinctive elements in mainline Jewish thought is the expectation that all these things will come about in this world, not in the next. The typical Jewish concern for this life is a thread which runs throughout the Jewish scriptures, at least until apocalyptic writing really comes into its own with the second-century book of Daniel. This book, on the other hand, points the way to a significant deviation from the standard faith, thanks to its preoccupation with the last days and its apocalyptic style. Yet even here it is still perfectly possible to understand 'the end of all things' and the promised golden age as being set in this world. After all, the earth is not destroyed in Daniel.

It may be because the end is seen in earthly terms that the figure of a Messiah (or saviour) – a powerful human figure who will bring this about – becomes more and more important. It is the Messiah who above all will enable the dispersed Jews to return to their own country. Christians often dismiss Jewish expectations of the Messiah at the time of Christ as being merely political. They will argue that Jesus' contemporaries failed to recognize him as their Messiah because their vision was not broad enough – because they were expecting an active military leader who would simply drive out the forces of the Roman occupation. This seems to me to be a simplistic view of Jewish expectation in the first century. It is also one that gives no acknowledgment to the way Jewish hopes had built up over the centuries since the exile, until by Jesus' day the long expectation of the Messiah had reached bursting point. Nor does it recognize how these hopes and expectations have continued down the centuries. To try to clarify my understanding of Jewish teaching on the messianic end-times I looked at the work of the medieval teacher Moses Maimonides, who at the end of the twelfth century formulated what he saw as the key principles of the Jewish faith.

Maimonides has this to say of the Jews' eventual return to their own land:

> The days of the Messiah will be the time when the kingdom will revert to Israel who will return to the Holy Land. The King who will then reign will have Zion as the capital of his realm... There is no difference between this world and the days of the Messiah except the subjugation of the kingdom alone.

When that happens, the rebuilding of the Temple and the restoration of ancient beliefs and the old law will follow. Other nations will be converted, but above all, Israel will be free to live in peace, enabling her people to devote themselves to the study of God's law. The Messiah is not immortal, but when he dies his reign will be continued by his descendants.

Maimonides returns several times to his key theme that nothing else will change: the world will go on as usual. Yet there does have to be change. With the Messianic age comes a new golden age where, because of the absence of conflict and obedience to God's law, life becomes easier:

> In those days the gaining of their livelihood will be so very easy to men that they will do the lightest possible labour and reap great benefit. [Hence the Rabbinical saying] 'The land of Israel will one day produce cakes ready baked and garments of fine silk.'

The Garden of Eden has in a sense been restored in those last days.

But Maimonides' thought has moved on from that of the Jewish scriptures. He saw this golden age on earth as a preparation for the state of bliss in the world to come after death. There is no threat of judgment and retribution: all Jews will share in this bliss, including sinners, unless they have renounced their faith. The resurrection of the dead (included in apocalyptic writing and hotly debated in the time of Christ) finds its place in this scheme of things as it becomes a spiritual rather than a bodily resurrection.

Nonetheless, the dominant Jewish view, even in the twelfth century AD, is of universal peace and happiness in this world rather than the next. Those who looked to apocalyptic events as a prelude to the end have always been a minority, usually members of apocalyptic sects. And if those sects, like the Essenes, believed that a Messiah might already have come, then they were bound to reformulate their ideas about the end-time.

Apocalyptic story-telling

It is one thing for a prophet to draw on apocalyptic themes and images in order to make a point effectively. It is quite another when those themes are the main purpose of the writing and the images are the means by which such themes are expressed. When this happens we have moved out of prophecy and into a form which is first and foremost a type of literature with its own special conventions – conventions that are regularly followed by its writers. This literature, whose influence extends to the present day and permeates contemporary culture, is represented in the Jewish scriptures by the second half of Zechariah and, especially, by the book of Daniel. And these books are followed by many more works of Jewish apocalyptic in the 200 years or so between Daniel and the fall of Jerusalem in AD70.

In order to be classed as a specific type (or 'genre') of literature, a piece of writing will have certain features which readers easily recognize as being characteristic of the style in question. So, for example, an autobiography will be written in the first person, by a real person who is telling his or her own story. A poem will have a different layout on the printed page from prose; it will depend on sound (often rhyme) for its effect, and will make use of metaphor or some other form of figurative language. Apocalyptic has its own distinctive features. Not every text will have all of them, but all will have some of them. It is defined both by its subject-matter and by its style.

The subject-matter of apocalyptic writing is of course the events at the end of the age. But in order to describe them convincingly, writers commonly follow the convention that they are revealed in a vision, usually to a great figure from the past, who is also said to have written the book. Daniel is one such visionary; Enoch is another. By the second century BC Enoch, who is described in Genesis 5:24 as one who 'walked with God', was being portrayed as a superhuman figure with special wisdom and knowledge. The visionary is also given an interpreter, usually an angel or archangel, who will reveal the meaning of the 'hidden things'. In Daniel 9 the interpreter is Gabriel, who says to him: 'O Daniel, I have now come out to give you wisdom and understanding' (Daniel 9:22). In 1 Enoch it is the archangel Uriel who acts as both guide and interpreter:

> I have shown you everything, O Enoch, and have revealed everything to you, that you may see this sun and this moon, and those who lead the stars of heaven... But in the days of the sinners the years will become shorter... and all things on the earth will change, and will not appear at their proper time (1 Enoch 80:1, 2, 3).

The Testament of Levi introduces an unnamed angel, charged with interceding for Israel, who takes Levi into the presence of God: 'The angel opened to me the gates of heaven, and I saw the holy temple, and the Most High sitting on a throne of glory' (5:1). Angels by now have assumed a key role in apocalyptic, and their presence from the second century BC onwards represents a new development in Jewish tradition.

Stylistically, apocalyptic writing is full of symbolism. This is perhaps inevitable, since symbols – where one thing stands for or represents another – add an extra level of meaning. And because the whole genre has to do with revealing knowledge of hidden things, beings, objects, events or ideas may all be given a new meaning in order to make known what is concealed. So the four beasts in Daniel 7 symbolize four kingdoms, and the ten horns of the fourth beast represent ten kings, although the identification is vague enough to allow them to be interpreted as various rulers in real life. Number symbolism is also important, and again it is open to changing interpretations. The prime numbers 3, 5 and 7 are particularly prone to such treatment. Measures of time are expressed in the vaguest of terms: 'they shall be given into his hand for a time, two times and half a time' (Daniel 7:25). The signs of the end – which particularly reflect the overthrowing of the natural order – are presented in various ways, all easily recognizable as characteristic of apocalyptic: stars fall from heaven, nations are ravaged by war, there is a great final conflict between good and evil.

What leads people to write in such a distinctive style? It is often said that apocalyptic emerges at a time of national crisis. After all, it is not usual, nor very healthy, to brood about the end of the world when everything is going well. But in a time of great upheaval apocalyptic may help people to make sense of what is going on around them. This is certainly true of the historical background to biblical and intertestamental apocalyptic. The Revelation of St John, for instance, is born out of a time of intense persecution for the early church. Wars, plagues and revolutions in medieval and modern times have all produced their share of apocalyptic thinking.

Nonetheless, the emergence of Jewish apocalyptic cannot be dissociated from popular developments in the Jewish religion, even though these may also have some connection with what was going on at the time. The most significant development is the growing belief in the resurrection of the dead and the implications this has for life after death.

The Jewish scriptures teach that death is final: believers are to concentrate on leading a good life in this world. And if anyone doubts that, then they are referred to Deuteronomy, 'The secret things belong to the Lord our God' (Deuteronomy 29:29), which effectively prohibits speculation about the future. The Mishnah (the teaching of the Law independently of its scriptural basis) has no description of the world to come, nor what Abba Hillel Silver calls 'the symbolic trivia characteristic of an apocalypse'. Death had to be accepted with resignation, as part of God's plan for humanity. Yet by the second century BC there was widespread belief in resurrection and some kind of immortality. Silver says this is not to be attributed to spiritual evolution. Indeed such a development was resisted because of a perceived association with the polytheistic beliefs of the Egyptians. Rather, it is due to the Jewish leaders' inability to withstand popular pressure, which came especially from Jews living outside Palestine who were susceptible to the influence of other religions.

There are occasional references to resurrection in the Jewish scriptures, which are generally held to be late additions, such as this verse in Isaiah:

> Thy dead shall live, their bodies shall rise.
> O dwellers in the dust, awake and sing for joy!
> For thy dew is a dew of light,
> and on the land of the shades thou wilt let it fall (Isaiah 26:19).

The non-canonical book of 2 Maccabees, on the other hand, which probably dates from the first century BC, celebrates Jewish martyrs and refers to their life after death: 'Our brothers after enduring a brief suffering have drunk of everflowing life under God's Covenant' (2 Maccabees 7:36).

By the second century AD the rabbis had banned all apocalyptic literature except for the book of Daniel. Nonetheless, the doctrine of resurrection did eventually become established in Rabbinic Judaism, although it was regarded as a secondary belief rather than a key principle.

Full-blown apocalyptic passes from Jewish to Christian writing in a virtually seamless progression. While the book of Revelation could be nothing other than a Christian work, many of the apocalypses written in the intertestamental period might be either Jewish or Christian compositions, or even a bit of both, as some Christian writers adopt established Jewish conventions with little or no modification. Yet once the persecutions of Jews and Christians begin to die down, at least temporarily, and the expectations of the Messiah's coming or of Christ's return have abated somewhat, literary apocalypse also fades from the scene. Writers revert to the older practice of selecting elements from apocalyptic style to lend emphasis to their own convictions.

Some characteristics of apocalyptic survive more obviously than others – in particular the lists of signs of the end that are included in prophetic warnings down the centuries or the intricate games with numbers to predict the events of the end. But other elements crop up in wider contexts. Angels and assorted apocalyptic symbols become commonplaces of Christian art. Then there is the solitary figure to whom the secrets of the end are revealed. It does not require too much imagination to see him as the forerunner of later heroes: the solitary survivor in Mary Shelley's *The Last Man* and the lone adventurer of *The Time Machine* and *2001 – A Space Odyssey*.

Crisis in the second century BC

The earliest example of fully fledged Jewish apocalyptic is the book of Daniel, or at least half of it. The book is in two parts: the adventures of Daniel himself, who lived through the Babylonian exile (chapters 1–6), and his apocalyptic dreams (chapters 7–12). It is, incidentally, a failure to recognize these dreams of a hero from the past as a literary convention that has led some commentators to insist that the whole book is what, on the face of it, it purports to be: the exploits of a sixth-century prophet. The stories of the first part, though, are a justification for using Daniel as the mouthpiece in the second part. He is shown to be wise and God-fearing, and a gifted interpreter of other people's dreams. In Daniel 10 it is stressed that he is set apart to receive special visions: 'I, Daniel, alone saw the vision... and when I heard the sound of his words, I fell on my face in a deep sleep' (Daniel 10:8, 9).

Daniel's visions, recorded in chapters 7 to 12, were to have a deep and lasting influence on Christian writers in particular, for two reasons. The first has to do with the symbolism of the dreams and the very precise identification with real events to which it has always given rise. In Daniel 7, the four great beasts which come out of the sea symbolize the final kingdoms before the end. The first beast was a lion with the wings of an eagle, and it is easy to see this as a symbol for Babylon, where winged lions were commonly represented. The remaining beasts were originally taken to represent the kingdoms of Media, Persia and Greece, but the second kingdom soon came to be reinterpreted as Medo-Persia, so that Rome could become the fourth kingdom.

More significant, though, for those who are not trying to match symbols and reality, is Daniel's vision of the eternal kingdom of the Son of Man (7:13-14), which is taken up by Jesus in his teaching on his return at the end of time: 'They will see the Son of man coming on the clouds of heaven with power and great glory' (Matthew 24:30).

The events which form the background to the book are well documented. The ruler in Palestine between 175 and 164BC was the Greek tyrant Antiochus IV, who called himself Epiphanes (the name means 'god manifest'). Antiochus' persecution of the Jews led to the plunder of the Jerusalem temple in 169BC, as it is described in 1 Maccabees:

> He took the table for the bread of the Presence, the cups for drink offerings, the bowls, the golden censers, the curtain, the crowns, and the gold decoration on the front of the temple; he stripped it all off. He took the silver and the gold, and the costly vessels; he took also the hidden treasures which he found. Taking them all, he departed to his own land. He committed deeds of murder, and spoke with great arrogance (1 Maccabees 1:22-24).

Two years later he ordered the Jews to give up their religion: 'They were to make themselves abominable by everything unclean and profane, so that they should forget the law and change all the ordinances' (1 Maccabees 1:48-49). Antiochus completed his desecration of the Temple by erecting there an altar to Zeus. For the Jews this was the last straw, and the years 167 to 164 were a period of bitter rebellion, in which the forces of Judas Maccabeus were eventually victorious.

The desecration of the Temple is referred to in Daniel 11: 'They shall set up the abomination that makes desolate' (v. 31) as part of the interpretation of Daniel's dream. But Antiochus is more than just a historical instance of a persecutor of the Jews. He has become a model for the tyrannical ruler who is to come at the end of time.

Qumran: Living in an eschatological community

Readers of the London *Times* on Monday 12 April 1948 could have been forgiven for overlooking a couple of column inches on page 4 under the title 'Ancient Manuscripts Found in Palestine'. The main overseas news that day was of tightening Soviet controls over access from the West to East Germany and Berlin, and of the Soviet Union's veto on Italy joining the United Nations. At home the British army had beaten the French army six-nil in a rugby match at Twickenham, while the England football team notched up a two-nil victory over Scotland at Hampden Park.

Yet the discovery of three scrolls including the earliest known manuscript of the Book of Isaiah, as well as some hitherto unknown non-biblical writings, was described by the same newspaper sixteen months later as 'the most important find ever made in Palestine'. The Dead Sea Scrolls, as they soon came to be known, were not only of considerable archaeological and historical importance. They revealed much about a Jewish sect who, around the time of Christ, were actively looking forward to the end of time.

The scrolls had actually been found the previous year. According to the writer of a later and more substantial *Times* article (published on 9 August 1949) a goatherd stumbled across a 'small circular opening in a rock face', in the foothills near the Dead Sea at Qumran. Hoping to discover golden treasure he found instead 'a treasure far greater than any found'. The first report of the find was published in an American archaeological journal in the summer of 1948, by which time, the *Times* writer noted, the British had withdrawn from Palestine and 'the tragedy and chaos of war reigned everywhere'.

When excavation of the site finally began in March 1949 there was considerable disagreement as to the date and significance of the treasures. The cautious warned that the scrolls might be medieval forgeries, and while the main body of opinion favoured an early date, opinion was divided as to whether this might be as early as the second century BC or as late as the second century AD. The jars in which the scrolls were found suggested the earlier dating, but there is no reason to suppose that they were brand new when they were used to house the scrolls. But whatever the precise date – and the majority of scholars now seem to favour the earlier option – one of the most intriguing questions is why the scrolls should have been there at all. What sort of community hid its treasured writings in huge Greek pots and stashed them away in a remote cave?

It is generally assumed that the scrolls belonged to the Essenes, a Jewish sect whose members followed a strict ascetic lifestyle in the belief that this would hasten the Day of the Lord. It was once thought that John the Baptist and even Jesus himself were Essenes, and since the discovery of the scrolls this idea is again proving attractive. Their life seems to have been made more difficult by persecution – the most likely reason for the elaborate precautions taken to protect their religious writings. In the end the whole community was wiped out, leaving no one to return to retrieve the scrolls from their rocky hiding place. This may have happened during the Roman persecution of AD70, which also destroyed the Jerusalem temple, although there were other persecutions both before and after that date. Since the cave also contained two lamps and a cooking pot of later Roman origin, it is tempting to believe that these may have belonged to the people who hid the scrolls away for the last time.

The Jewish historian Josephus, in his account of the Jewish War of AD66–70, describes the Essenes' strict observance of Jewish law and their confidence that eternal life would follow immediately after death:

Teaching the same doctrine as the sons of Greece, they declare that for the good souls there waits a home beyond the ocean, a place troubled by neither rain nor snow nor heat, but refreshed by the zephir that blows ever gentle from the ocean. Bad souls they consign to a darksome, stormy abyss, full of punishments that know no end.

Josephus then adds, almost as an afterthought:

Some of them claim to foretell the future, after a lifelong study of sacred literature, purifications of different kinds, and the aphorisms of prophets; rarely if ever do their predictions prove wrong.

The Qumran documents as we have them do not contain the dramatic descriptions of the end of time that characterize other writing of the same period, though these must have formed part of the background to their beliefs. The fragmentary nature of many parts of the scrolls, coupled with the fact that writers do not bother setting down things that are too obvious or too integral a part of daily life to restate, means that we do not know all the details of how the Essenes viewed the future. Even so there are plenty of clues to suggest that they were far more preoccupied with such things than mainstream Jews.

One important clue is in the texts the community valued. No fewer than eleven manuscript copies of 1 Enoch were produced for Qumran between the second century BC and the first century AD. The fragments of twelve manuscripts of the book of Jubilees were found there – the book in which Enoch is chosen by God to foresee the future up to the last judgment and which Qumran's Damascus Document cites as authoritative. A further clue is to be found in the Essenes' commentaries on Old Testament texts which are interpreted in terms of events at the end of time. One example is the commentary on Isaiah 11:1–3 ('A shoot will come up from the stump of Jesse…'): '[This concerns the Branch] of David who shall arise at the end [of days]… he shall rule over all the [nations]… and his sword shall judge [all] the peoples.' There are also collections of texts about the Messiah and a 'Midrash [collection of texts] on the Last Days'. In this, Psalm 2:2 ('The kings of the earth take their stand and the rulers gather together against the Lord and against his Anointed One') is glossed as concerning the kings 'who shall [rage against] the elect of Israel in the last days'.

There are other peculiarly distinctive features of Essene belief. The most striking is the way in which their hope is centred on a historical person, known as the Teacher of Righteousness, 'to whom God made known all the mysteries of the words of his servants the prophets'. The Teacher, thought to have begun his ministry around 155 BC, appears to have built up the Qumran Community. The scrolls reveal an expectation that he will return, perhaps as a prophet or as a priestly Messiah. It is unclear, though, whether this figure would emerge from the existing world order or would appear as an eschatological being at the end of time. The picture is further complicated by contemporary Jewish belief in two Messiahs – one of whom was expected to come from the line of priests (descended from Aaron). But whatever the precise nature of the once and future Teacher of Righteousness, the centrality of a figure from the past to whom future hopes are attached is an important development, and one to which we shall return.

Another thing which makes the Essenes distinctive is a conviction that is typical of any sect as opposed to mainstream religion: that their particular community had been chosen to be a righteous community set apart to be saved. This emerges clearly from the commentary on Habakkuk 2:1-2, in which the Community see themselves as the final generation: 'God told Habakkuk to write down that which would happen to the final generation, but he did not make known to him when time would come to an end. And as for that which he said, *That he who reads may read it speedily*, interpreted this concerns the Teacher of Righteousness.' This train of thought is continued in the comment on Habakkuk 2:4 ('But the righteous shall live by his faith'): 'Interpreted, this concerns all those who observe the Law in the House of Judah, whom God will deliver from the House of Judgment because of their suffering and because of their faith in the Teacher of Righteousness.'

Underlying Essene teaching is a kind of dualism. According to the *Community Rule*, God has put two spirits in the world – of truth and falsehood – which are both at work in the human heart, struggling for supremacy. Consequently human beings 'walk in both wisdom and folly', their eternal future dependent on 'the spirit within [them at the time] of the visitation'. Those inclined to righteousness are promised 'healing, great peace in a long life, and fruitfulness, together with every everlasting blessing and eternal joy in life without end, a crown of glory and a garment of majesty in unending light'. This is combined with the picture of a cleansing, purifying God, who will wipe away all misdeeds and falsehood from those who are predominantly righteous. For those who are above all ruled by falsehood, though, there is a grim future in store:

> The visitation of all who walk in this spirit shall be a multitude of plagues by the hand of all the destroying angels, everlasting damnation by the avenging wrath of the fury of God, eternal torment and endless disgrace together with shameful extinction in the fire of the dark regions. The times of all their generations shall be spent in sorrowful mourning and in bitter misery and in calamities of darkness until they are destroyed without remnant or survivor.

The apocalyptic terrors foreseen by the prophet Joel and others are here related to the individual, but the outcome for them at the end of the age is no different.

If the struggle between the spirits of truth and falsehood is centred in people's hearts, it is also enacted at the cosmic level in a battle between the Sons of Light and the Sons of Darkness. The personal and the universal are intertwined: the Community believed that it would win through such turbulent times still on this earth in order to attack the occupiers of the Holy Land and to regain Jerusalem. In the seventh year of that war Temple worship would be restored through their efforts, but before that could happen the Community had met its end.

The Essenes were one of only two communities of believers 2,000 years ago whose faith could be said to be eschatological. The others were the Christians. The Qumran Community were completely obliterated, while the Christians had no choice but to make a clean break with Judaism, which, in the words of Abba Hillel Silver, 'saw in Christianity... a fatal eschatological overemphasis' as well as a perceived weakening of the belief in a single God, once he was believed to have taken human form in the person of Jesus. Was this then the end of Jewish apocalyptic?

Quietly waiting

Looking at later developments in Jewish eschatological belief alongside Christian ones, it is tempting to try to make connections. For example, times of turmoil, when Christians have thought they have seen signs of the end have also been times when some Jewish communities have experienced prophetic outbursts, predicting the coming of the Messiah. Ironically and tragically, Christian expectation has sometimes fostered such prophetic activity, particularly in the highly charged anti-Semitic atmosphere of the Middle Ages which included the belief that Antichrist would be born of a Jewish mother.

Ruth Gladstein has stressed the shift in Jewish messianic attitudes from violent activity in the years of the first-century Roman persecution to a quieter, more introverted messianism which lasted into medieval times and beyond. Although the longing for the Messiah has always remained, it has only rarely given rise to any form of militant action. Gladstein cites one possible example of this which also has a Christian connection. It is the episode in the 1419 'crusade' against the Christian Hussites of Bohemia when the Pope's crusaders also attacked Bohemian Jews. The Hussites (a Christian reform movement) seem to have believed that the end was near, and the fact that they were aligning themselves with Jews is taken as an indication that the latter were also anticipating the end.

Many Jews expected that the Messiah would appear in the fifth century, that is 400 years after the destruction of the Temple in AD70. This hope was fuelled by Christian predictions of the rise of Antichrist when Rome fell to Visigothic invaders in 410, and the expectation of Christ's return in the years that followed. In the event all that happened was that a messianic pretender on the island of Crete led local Jews into the sea like a second Moses, anticipating a repetition of the miracle at the Red Sea. Otherwise it was moments of particular persecution that inspired brief reappearances of eschatological hope among the Jews. This was notable in eighth-century Persia at the time of the Islamic conquests, and again during the period of the medieval crusades. In Europe such events as the expulsion of the Jews from Spain in 1492 led to widespread belief that the Messiah would seek vengeance, while anti-Jewish measures taken during the Italian Counter-Reformation in the 1560s led to the hope that this might represent the birth-pangs of the Messiah.

In his study of Jewish religious movements, Stephen Sharot concludes that these bursts of millenarian activity were short-lived and largely confined to particular areas. Yet the quiet Jewish hope remains. Some years ago I translated a collection of Jewish prayers from an Italian compilation, and was struck by the song which traditionally concludes the Passover prayers. It is a prayer for the Day of the Messiah:

> May the time draw near
> when there will be neither night nor day!
> Help us, O God, to understand
> that the day is yours
> and the night is yours also.
> Place guards in your holy city
> to stay there both day and night.
> Make the darkness of night
> shine in the brilliant light
> of your day.

References

Jacob I. Dienstag (editor), *Eschatology in Maimonidean Thought: Messianism, Resurrection and the World to Come: Selected Studies*, Bibliotheca Maimonidica, vol. 2, Ktar Publishing House, 1983.

Ruth Gladstein, 'Eschatological Trends in Bohemian Jewry during the Hussite Period', in A. Williams (editor), *Prophecy and Millenarianism (Essays in Honour of Marjorie Reeves)*, Longman, 1980.

Josephus (translated by G.A. Williamson), *The Jewish War*, Penguin Books, 1959.

Elias Kopciowski (translated by Paula Clifford), *Praying with the Jewish Tradition*, Triangle Books, 1988.

Stephen Sharot, *Messianism, Mysticism and Magic: A Sociological Analysis of Jewish Religious Movements*, University of North Carolina Press, Chapel Hill, 1982.

Abba Hillel Silver, *Where Judaism Differs: An Inquiry into the Distinctiveness of Judaism*, 1956; London, Collier Macmillan, 1989.

Gaza Vermes, *The Dead Sea Scrolls in English*, Penguin Books, 1962.

Chapter 3

Longing for the End

'Beyond question Jesus threatened like all the prophets.
But he did it in a remarkable new way. He did not
threaten with the judgment of God but with the judgment
of the mysterious "Man". No one was certain of
withstanding his judgment. But everyone had a chance.'

Gerd Theissen, *The Shadow of the Galilean*

These are the words of a distinguished New Testament scholar, a Professor
at the University of Heidelberg. But the context is not a scholarly book or
article, or even a sermon. Gerd Theissen's *The Shadow of the Galilean* is more
like a novel, even though it has a serious purpose. Although Jesus himself
never appears in person the aim of the book is to show us what it was like to
be a Jew in first-century Palestine, to present the historical, religious and
political circumstances in which Jesus of Nazareth lived, worked and died.

As I have already started to demonstrate, there was no shortage of
speculation in Jesus' time as to when the end of the world might come. This
of course hardly endeared Palestinian Jews to their Roman masters.
Theissen has his narrator go in search of the Qumran community, ostensibly
as a spy reporting back to the Romans, and he says this:

> I did not write that the Essenes hated the Romans. They indeed
> repudiated armed rebellion in the present, dreaming instead of a great
> war at the end of time. Then along with all the children of light, they
> would conquer and destroy the children of darkness. The only
> question was when they would come to feel that the last days were
> upon them. Then they could be dangerous.

The teaching of Jesus on the end was at once a reflection of the thought of his time, as Theissen reports it, and yet vitally different from it. In order to appreciate the distinctiveness of Christian thought we need to begin with the words and actions of Jesus himself. This is not as straightforward as it might appear. The gospels which provide us with accounts of Jesus' life and teaching did not begin to be written until a good thirty years after Jesus' death, resurrection and ascension. By then there was no question of Christianity being just another Jewish sect: it was a rival religion. By then too, the early Christians were beginning to feel the effects of persecution, which intensified after AD70 when they were suspected of being involved in the devastation of Jerusalem.

By the time the gospels were written the first disciples, who had understood Jesus' promise that he would return to mean a return in the near future, were old, if not already dead. For them there was previously little point in writing down anything about Jesus, since everyone was convinced the end was very near. Little wonder then that when those accounts were actually written, the evangelists were concerned to use Jesus' words to reassure the new Christian churches that the promised end was still not far off. They also viewed the events of Jesus' life from the perspective of the Jewish scriptures, in order to prove, or at least to imply, that Jesus was indeed the saviour whom all Israel expected. So the faithful were encouraged to see their own difficult times as the persecutions which heralded the end. I do not mean to imply that the gospel writers were being in any way untruthful in their records; rather that the emphasis they put on Jesus' words reflected the concerns of their day. An example will make this clear.

The gospels of Matthew and Mark have Jesus using the language of Daniel 9:27 in describing in fairly general terms one of the events of the end – the desecration of holy places: 'When you see the desolating sacrilege set up where it ought not to be... then let those who are in Judea flee to the mountains' (Mark 13:14). Luke, on the other hand, is more specific: 'When you see Jerusalem surrounded by armies, then know that its desolation is near. Then let those who are in Judea flee...' (Luke 21:20-21). Luke's readers had already seen Jerusalem surrounded by armies in AD70, so clearly the end had to be near. While the other two writers keep to the original general prophecy, Luke draws the inference which to him must have been obvious. He goes on to develop the idea of the suffering of 'this people': 'they will fall by the sword and be led captive among all nations; and Jerusalem will be trodden down by the Gentiles, until the times of the

Gentiles are fulfilled' (Luke 21:24). These concerns and interpretations need to be recognized at the outset, because as Christian history develops new expectations and interpretations will be added to them.

Given the widespread Jewish expectation in the time of Jesus that the time of the Messiah is near, it is not surprising that we read of Jesus' disciples asking him not whether the world will end but when. Yet the bulk of Jesus' teaching has to do with neither of these questions. It focuses instead on the type of behaviour that will enable ordinary people, irrespective of race, sex or social class, to be judged to be among the 'righteous' when the end comes. And it is those who are merciful, pure in heart, peacemakers, those who are ready to suffer persecution on account of Christ, who will fall into this category. Jesus' teaching also lays down new ground rules for community behaviour, such that the 'kingdom of heaven' may be attainable at least to some degree in this life as well as in the next, for all those who respond to him.

The person of Jesus is at the heart of his message: 'I have come as light into the world, that whoever believes in me may not remain in darkness' (John 12:46). Time and again would-be disciples are told 'follow me', while the promise of life after death is inseparable from the promise of being with Jesus himself: 'When I go and prepare a place for you, I will come again and will take you to myself, that where I am you may be also.' So too the person of Jesus is at the centre of all that he teaches in relation to the end.

'Thy kingdom come'

The line from the Lord's Prayer raises a problem that makes Jesus' teaching on the end quite distinct from anything that had gone before. In the course of his ministry Jesus revealed to those who would listen that he was the Messiah whom the Jews were so eagerly expecting. When John the Baptist in prison gets people to go and ask Jesus 'Are you he who is to come, or shall we look for another?' (Matthew 11:3), Jesus confirms to them that John is the prophet referred to in Malachi 3:1 who has been sent to prepare the way before him, that is, Jesus. But if Jesus has come as the prophesied Messiah, then surely he should also be bringing about the new age, if not the actual end-time? Clearly this is not so, as Jesus' teaching looks to the future, to the time when he will himself return in glory. Modern theologians, following C.H. Dodd, have tended to refer to this paradox as 'realized eschatology', meaning that Christians are already living in the end-times which began with Jesus' first coming. It is not hard to see from this how some people have been eager to put a specific time limit on this preparatory period, and have been more than willing to try and fix a date for Jesus' return.

There is, though, nothing in Jesus' own words to support this. As we have already seen, the early church taught that his return would be sooner rather than later, stressing Jesus' statement that 'this generation will not pass away before all these things take place' (Mark 13:30). However, this is to overlook the teaching that follows immediately afterwards: 'Of that day or that hour no one knows, not even the angels in heaven, nor the Son, but only the Father' (Mark 13:32). This comment has led some commentators to suppose that the 'this generation' saying refers only to the fall of Jerusalem, while others suggest that it confirms Jesus' saying that even he did not know the time of the end.

Jesus' words and actions

Jesus' main teaching on the end of the age is contained in the so-called 'little apocalypse' of Mark 13, Matthew 24 and Luke 21. It begins with a prophecy of the fall of Jerusalem: 'There will not be left here one stone upon another, that will not be thrown down' (Mark 13:2). This leads four of the disciples to ask Jesus privately, 'When will this be and what will be the sign when those things are all to be accomplished?' (13:4). Since what follows is all about the end of the age and not just the end of the Jerusalem Temple, there is inevitably some loss of understanding. Did the disciples ask about one thing (the Temple) and Jesus tell them about another (the end of the age) or was it the other way round? Were they all referring to one or the other? The writer has assumed we know something that after such a lapse of time of course we don't. Did the end of the Temple automatically mean the end of the world, at least for a certain group of people? Or not?

The passage that follows seems fairly typical of an apocalyptic style, or is it? Jesus did not write anything down, so there is already a departure from tradition: apocalyptic, usually a style of literary writing, has suddenly been presented as a manner of speaking. Then there are the signs – familiar ones from the Jewish prophets, together with two new ones: the faithful will be persecuted (v. 9) and the end cannot come before the good news of Christ has been preached 'to all nations' (v. 10). It has been demonstrated, notably by David Wenham, that the 'little apocalypse' was in circulation as an independent element well before the synoptic gospels which incorporated it were compiled. This implies that the discourse was being used as a means of teaching Christian doctrine within a very short time of Christ's resurrection. It is a compelling argument, because it reflects clearly the atmosphere in which the new faith was spreading: much of Judaism was caught up in the expectation that the end was near, and now the Christian message was confirming it.

The traditional language of apocalyptic used in these passages has lost something: the emphasis on almost wanton destruction. Certainly the end is to be feared, but the terrors are downplayed in the context of a more optimistic message. Given the Jewish expectation at the time of Christ that the end was near, Jesus' teaching offers an alternative to resignation in the face of a wrathful God. This is the promise of a new rule of peace, fufiling ancient prophecy and brought about through God's Son's love for humankind and sustained by their love for him and for one another.

Supplementing Jesus' words are his actions. The idea that what you do carries as much meaning as what you say was a familiar one at the time. Jesus' first followers knew the Jewish prophets; they knew very well that Jeremiah had bought a piece of land just before the Babylonians invaded, as a sign from God that one day the country would be returned to its inhabitants and they would be able to buy 'houses and fields and vineyards' there (Jeremiah 32:15). They knew too how Hosea had married and remained loving to a wife who was to be unfaithful to him, thereby symbolizing God's faithful relationship with his people. This was another action rich in meaning and commanded by God: 'Go take to yourself a wife of harlotry and have children of harlotry, for the land commits great harlotry by forsaking the Lord' (Hosea 1:2). So when Jesus – after his baptism by John, an acknowledged prophet – chose twelve men to be his disciples, his action too had a deeper meaning. It became an allusion to the twelve tribes of Israel who had been scattered but were now being brought together around the person of Christ. It is a prophetic action and a sign of the end-times. Many other actions of Jesus are singled out as having a special meaning beyond their immediate contexts, particularly in the gospel of John: the changing of water into wine at a marriage celebration, the miraculous feeding of thousands of people, and the raising of Lazarus who had been dead for three days.

The gospel writers are at pains to stress the continuity between Jewish scriptures and Jesus; they point to events that can be taken to symbolize a new beginning in Israel's history which is marked by Jesus' birth and which will lead to 'the consolation of Israel' — the fulfilling of Jewish hopes and expectation. The incident in Luke 2 in which a devout, expectant Jew called Simeon blesses the infant Jesus, symbolizes both this continuity and this fulfilment: 'Mine eyes have seen thy salvation which thou hast prepared in the presence of all peoples, a light for revelation to the Gentiles and for glory to thy people Israel' (vv. 30-32).

Jesus' teaching about the timing of the end also differs from that of his contemporaries. Whereas Jewish apocalyptic sets out to reveal cosmic mysteries and lists both the signs and the events of the end-time, Jesus' teaching mostly takes all that as read. Instead he majors on what the attitude of his followers must be in the light of all these things. It is a simple message: they must be always alert, always ready for the end and for God's judgment.

What could easily sound bleak and severe is lightened by the parables Jesus told in order to put his message across. There is, for example, the story often referred to as 'the wise and foolish virgins' in Matthew 25. Ten girls wait to escort the bridegroom to his waiting bride. This would normally have happened during the hours of daylight — there was no need for any other form of light. But on this occasion the bridegroom (a common metaphor for Jesus himself) was late and five of the girls who had no oil for their lamps were taken by surprise. By the time they had sorted themselves out it was too late — the marriage feast had begun and they were shut out. Because, in Jesus' words, no one knows when the end will come except God alone, Christians are told to be prepared for the end, and for judgment, however unlikely its coming may seem. This has always been the standard teaching of the Christian church. As Bishop Ken's hymn puts it:

Redeem thy mis-spent time that's past
And live this day as if thy last;
Improve thy talent with due care;
For the great day thyself prepare.

The end delayed

There was little doubt in the minds of the first Christians after Jesus' resurrection and ascension that he would return and bring history to an end. When this did not happen, a new idea comes to the fore on the eschatological scene: the concept of a delay. Delay has to do with a temporary failure of expectations: a planned event fails to materialize at the time when it is expected, but there is no question of it not taking place eventually. Such a view attributes a role to those who wait. Previously the actors in the drama of the end had been God himself, his prophets or angelic messengers, and the people who heard the unwelcome message and who, hopefully, took appropriate action – preparing themselves or mending their ways. Christian eschatology adds further players: the people who are actively longing for the end.

The idea of delay is already present in a parable of Jesus, although since it is recorded only in Luke's gospel, it may well be a later reworking of another saying. In Luke 18 the gospel writer comments that the meaning of the parable is that Christians 'ought always to pray and not lose heart' – the implication being that the early church was indeed getting disheartened by the delay. The parable itself simply takes the picture of people continually begging God for the end to come and recasts it in the form of a widow who pesters a judge for judgment so much that eventually he gives in. Of course the widow had every right to expect a speedy outcome of her case; the delay is caused because the judge is a law unto himself: 'I neither fear God nor regard man' (18:4), yet in the end he does what is expected of him. How much more likely, then, is God to do the same:

> Will not God vindicate his elect, who cry to him day and night? Will he delay long over them? I tell you, he will vindicate them speedily. Nevertheless, when the Son of man comes, will he find faith on earth? (Luke 18:6-8).

Even here, though, there is an escape clause. Is the delay due to a lack of faith? Like Matthew, Luke ends his gospel with Jesus' commission to his disciples to preach 'repentance and forgiveness of sins... to all nations, beginning from Jerusalem', and this task is taken up in Luke's sequel, the Acts of the Apostles, which is the story of the early church. In a sermon recorded in Acts 3, the apostle Peter declares that the delay is deliberate: Christ will not return until faith in him has not only been preached, but preached successfully (Acts 3:19-21). Peter tells the Jewish people that they are the first to have received Christ; but the whole of God's original promise to Abraham, that 'all the families of the earth shall be blessed', has yet to be fulfilled.

There is no time scale set for the missionary activities of the early church, though it could not have been seen as covering a particularly long time. After all, a delay in the normal course of events is by definition a short period that is unlikely to extend beyond the foreseeable future. It makes little sense for me to say that if, for the sake of argument, I am in my twenties and unmarried, I am going to delay making a will until after my grandchildren are born. That is not so much a delay as an almost indefinite postponement, at least at the time of speaking. And postponement is something which Christian thinkers on eschatology rarely countenance.

There is a slightly different rationalization of the delay before the end in 2 Thessalonians. The writer argues (in chapter 2) that it is not possible for Christ to return unnoticed. Before that happens he must be preceded by 'the man of lawlessness, the son of perdition' (v. 3). That this has not yet taken place is thanks to a mysterious figure who is 'restraining' lawlessness, allowing the preaching of the gospel to continue in the interim. There is no indication what this figure may represent. It may be the Holy Spirit, or it may be, as modern commentators suggest, simply a reference to the binding of Satan. From Tertullian onwards, though, the Church Fathers saw it as a reference to the Roman state. Tertullian declares:

> A stupendous shock impends over the whole world and the very ending of the age threatening terrible sufferings; and this we know is only retarded by the respite won by the Roman empire. We have no wish to experience these calamities and as we pray that they may be delayed we favour the long-continued existence of Rome (*Apologeticus*, 32).

The delay would therefore last as long as the Roman empire, whose collapse would be followed by the rule of ten kings and Antichrist, as promised in Revelation 17.

How to wait

Once the idea of a delay was established, Christian writers had a further problem to tackle: how should people who believed they were already living in the end-time behave? How were they to live in a way that was distinctive and would mark them as different from those who had no such beliefs? On one level the teaching of Jesus was more than adequate as a model for the new community. But in some parts of the New Testament epistles, which put particular stress on this problem, the writers are at pains to show how Christ's teaching is to work out in practice.

The epistle of James urges patience:

> Be patient... until the coming of the Lord. Behold, the farmer waits for the precious fruit of the earth, being patient over it until it receives the early and the late rain... Establish your hearts, for the coming of the Lord is at hand (James 5:7–8).

The writer takes Jesus' command to be always prepared for the end and gives a practical example of the form that preparedness might take:

> Do not grumble... against one another, that you may not be judged; behold, the Judge is standing at the doors (v. 9).

Chapter 3 of 2 Peter – the last book to be accepted as part of the New Testament canon – is wholly concerned with Christ's return, both the fact of it and the time. The writer attributes the delay not to slowness on God's part, but to God's desire that everyone should be saved. The implication then is that Christians should be busy preaching repentance, and this introduces another idea which subsequently has been very popular in certain Protestant circles – that the coming of the end is in human hands: the actions of Christians can be 'hastening the coming of the day of God' (2 Peter 3:12). In the meantime Christians are exhorted to live lives of 'holiness and godliness' (v. 11) because when the time comes they are anxious to be found 'without spot or blemish and at peace' (v. 14).

The Pauline epistles betray a concern for the reputation of the young church. In Colossians 3 and elsewhere the apostle Paul shows his readers that they must order their personal relationships. Since the household was the basic unit of the state, the state's good order was dependent on a well-ordered family life. So he borrows from Jewish and Graeco-Roman culture a form of 'house rules': not only does order in personal relationships conform to the will of God, but it means that Christians will not be seen as in any way subversive, undermining the structures of current society.

The writer of the Epistle to the Hebrews is convinced that the end-time has begun: 'in these last days [God] has spoken to us by a Son, whom he appointed the heir of all things' (Hebrews 1:2). Perhaps acknowledging the difficulties faced by Christians under persecution, he encourages them not to let their hope waver and again offers some practical advice for day-to-day living:

> Let us consider how to stir up one another to love and good works, not neglecting to meet together, as is the habit of some, but encouraging one another, and all the more as you see the Day drawing near (Hebrews 10:24-25).

He encourages them to display the same confidence when times are easier as they seem to have done when they 'endured a hard struggle with sufferings' (v. 32) and quotes the prophet Habakkuk: 'For yet a little while, and the coming one shall come and shall not tarry' (v. 37).

Faith, confidence, encouragement of one another, and upright behaviour are all to mark the behaviour of those who live in the end-time and constitute a kind of ethics of the end. But the conviction remains for all these New Testament writers that they will not have very long to wait.

John's apocalypse

The book of Revelation, sometimes referred to as The Apocalypse, or the Revelation of St John the Divine, has had the most profound influence on eschatological thinking since it made its appearance at the end of the first century AD. The symbolism and mythological language in which much of the book is couched have affected the way both Christian and secular ideas on the end have been expressed right up to the present day.

It is clear from the very beginning that Revelation is a literary work in the tradition of Daniel and subsequent Jewish apocalyptic writing. John opens with the words 'The revelation [apocalypse] of Jesus Christ, which God gave him to show to his servants what must soon take place'. However, John's vision of the end is more complex than anything that has gone before, and his range of expression is widened accordingly. In John's writing we see literal and figurative language being pushed almost to breaking point as he attempts to convey a vision whose content is beyond words. Interpreters whose ingenuity might have been challenged by the symbolism of Daniel have had an absolute field day with Revelation.

John does not restrict himself to the conventional features of apocalyptic, inherited from his Jewish predecessors, although they are certainly present (for example, the details of the plagues in Revelation 16 elaborate some of the familiar signs of the end). Some of his pictures are modelled on the Old Testament prophets. So the vision of God's throne in Revelation 4:2-3 reflects Ezekiel 1:26-28, although unlike his predecessor John does not attempt to describe the form of God himself. His vision also shows prophecy being fulfilled, such as the defeat of Gog and his armies (Ezekiel 38:18) which is described in Revelation 20. In addition John draws on images or legends from Greek and Roman history and literature (including the legend that the dead Nero will return), while still more images are of his own creation. And in John too there appears a truly Christian eschatology with Christ – the Lamb who was slain – together with God the Father at the heart of it all.

A further level of meaning can be added by the social and historical context of the book of Revelation. The author of a sociolinguistic study has seen it as a product of social opposition, marked by 'an incessant verbal contest against ungodly forces', and using the language of believers who consistently oppose the devil and the Roman empire.

I shall come back to the book of Revelation frequently in considering the signs, times, people and interpretations of the end. It is a book which abounds in wonderful poetry, especially in the hymns of praise and the vision of a new heaven and a new earth. Yet, in the words of one commentator (who had Revelation 20 particularly in mind), it is 'the paradise of cranks and fanatics on the one hand and literalists on the other. It bristles with questions.' What is certain is that almost wherever one turns for ideas on the end of time, the Revelation of St John will be there somewhere.

Judgment

In the collegiate church of St Mary in Warwick there is a wall-painting of the Last Judgment. It dates from 1678 and adorns the Beauchamp Chapel, which houses the tombs of the fifteenth- and sixteenth-century earls of Warwick. On the left of the picture, on Christ's right hand, the faithful ascend to heaven, while on the other side sinners are despatched to hell. Originally, before the colours faded, it would have been a powerful visual aid, and historical events have made it even more powerful. In 1694 the fire of Warwick damaged the bottom area of hell on the right of the picture; so now the unhappy sinners descend into genuine obliteration, while the other side of the painting has survived gloriously without a mark.

The first centuries of the Christian era saw considerable development in thinking about the judgment that lay ahead at the end of time in both Jewish and Christian circles. Christian teaching closely reflects its Jewish origins, but is particularly linked to Jesus' picture of the sheep and the goats:

> When the Son of man comes in his glory, and all the angels with him, then he will sit on his glorious throne. Before him will be gathered all the nations, and he will separate them one from another as a shepherd separates the sheep from the goats, and he will place the sheep at his right hand, but the goats at the left (Matthew 25:31-33).

The separation depends on compassionate behaviour – feeding the hungry, visiting the sick – and the King says to the righteous: 'As you did it to the least of these my brethren, you did it to me.' Those on the King's right enter his kingdom; those on the left are sent into the fire of eternal punishment.

Revelation 20 portrays judgment as the opening up of books which record all that people have done on earth. The process is straightforward: 'If anyone's name was not found written in the book of life, he was thrown into the lake of fire' (Revelation 20:15). It is clear here that judgment takes place at the end of time, not on the death of the individual. So those who have died are resurrected for judgment, and if they are unworthy of eternal life they are condemned to 'the second death, the lake of fire' (v. 14). Of course this raised new questions – most particularly what happens between death and the final resurrection – which would occupy theologians for centuries to come.

Gradually over time the original biblical picture is made more elaborate. One popular additional detail is of souls being weighed in the balance, and artists develop it in their own way. In the National Museum of Catalan Art in Barcelona there is a splendid thirteenth-century altar frontal showing St Michael weighing a human head in one side of the balance, while a devil tries to cheat by pushing down on the other side.

A Christian heresy

Around AD170 the young Christian church was divided by the first of the apocalpytic sects that have sprung up at various times throughout its history.

Three charismatic prophets in Phrygia (in Central Asia Minor) proclaimed that Christ was about to return to reign on earth with his saints for 1,000 years. Following Revelation, they declared that the new holy city of Jerusalem would come down out of heaven, but – in the first of a series of new locations – claimed that on earth the new city would not be in Palestine but in Phrygia. The prophets – Montanus, Prisca and Maximilla – went further by insisting that Christians recognize them as having been chosen by the Holy Spirit and accept their prophecy as being of the Spirit.

Some characteristics of later sects are already evident in Montanism, such as the insistence that inspiration is given to individuals rather than to the leaders or hierarchy of the church, and consequently outrageous claims have been made for himself by the prophet and, indeed, for his own home town or local area. And of course division followed. Henry Chadwick concludes that the effect of Montanism was to 'reinforce the conviction that revelation had come to an end with the apostolic age, and so to foster the creation of a closed canon of the New Testament'. However, the existence of the New Testament in its fixed and final form is no barrier to later prophets making similar claims of themselves; and, given Christian belief in the continuing creative power of the Holy Spirit, it could hardly be otherwise.

The most famous supporter of the Montanists was the Latin theologian Tertullian. His conversion to their beliefs means that his works often contradict themselves, particularly when he is writing about the Holy Spirit and about the last things. So his early hope that the terrible events of the end might be delayed is later replaced by a longing for them:

> Our hope of the resurrection cannot be fulfilled, as I think, before the coming of Christ: and therefore all our prayers yearn for the passing of this age and the end of the world, at the great day of the Lord, the day of his wrath and retribution (*De Resurrectione Carnis*, 22).

The Church Fathers and Augustine

The so-called Fathers of the Church range from the immediate successors of the apostles, such as Clement of Rome or Ignatius of Antioch in the first and early second centuries, to the theologians of the fourth century, by which time the process of formulating more complex aspects of Christian doctrine and of defining important theological beliefs was well underway.

In the writings of the Fathers there is a general longing for the end and an insistence on the imminence of the end as promised in scripture. Clement of Rome takes this view and also stresses that there can be no escape from the judgment to come. He accompanies this with an encouragement to do good not evil:

> Let us fear [the Lord] and abandon hideous desires for evil deeds, that we may be sheltered by his mercy from the coming judgments. For where can any of us escape from his mighty hand? (First Epistle to the Corinthians, xxviii).

Some writers draw further on other traditions, such as a contempt for the present world (from pagan antiquity), or the purification of the soul by fire (from Zoroastrianism).

There is much speculation by early Christian theologians on the nature of resurrection and whether the resurrection body will be spiritual or bodily in form. Origen, writing in the first half of the third century, bases his arguments on passages in 1 Corinthians 15 and concludes:

> By the command of God the body which was earthly and animal will be replaced by a spiritual body, such as may be able to dwell in heaven... But even for those destined for eternal fire or for punishment there will be an incorruptible body through the change of the resurrection (De Principiis, II.x.3).

St Augustine's great work, The City of God, was begun in the year 413 and took him thirteen years to write. Originally he had intended to write a treatise arguing against the charge that Christians were to blame for the fall of Rome three years earlier, and showing that paganism contained the seeds of its own destruction. But what he ended up with was a much bigger theme, interpreting the whole of history as a struggle between good and evil. The two cities of the title are the pagan earthly city and the God-centred heavenly city.

We shall see later that this book effectively silenced the debates about when the end would come. But Augustine considers many other aspects of end-time, including the resurrection of the dead. In his theology there are two resurrections: the first is a spiritual resurrection that comes with baptism in this life, and the second is bodily resurrection at the end of time, 'which by the last judgment shall dismiss some into the second death, others into that life which has no death' (XX, 6).

Augustine also tackled the question of what happens between death and the end. His answer is that the saints – who have already undergone bodily resurrection – will be 'in upper regions', untouched by fire or flood (XX, 18):

> When they have become immortal and incorruptible they shall not greatly dread the blaze of that conflagration, as the corruptible and mortal bodies of the three men were able to live unhurt in the blazing furnace.

The reference is to the three young men in Daniel 6.

Unlike many who write on such topics, Augustine's greatness lies in his humility. In approaching questions which must have been circulating freely in the theological debates of his time, he is not afraid to say that he does not know. What happens to those who are alive when Christ returns? What will the day of judgment be like?

> If we are unable perfectly to comprehend the manner in which [resurrection] shall take place, our faith is not on this account vain.

Consequently, we can 'only feebly conjecture' how such things will happen, but Augustine is confident that we shall understand when they do.

What are we waiting for?

> And when they blow the final whistle
> When the final time is up
> I will stand before my Saviour
> And receive the winner's cup...
> (Sung to the theme tune of BBC's *Match of the Day*).

What exactly do Christians understand by that 'final time'? Is it the end of everything, or is it simply the end of the world as we currently know it? The song that puts it in footballing terms seems quite clear: the game (life) ends and the winners (the good team) are rewarded. End of story. And this is probably how most people – insofar as they think of such things at all – would describe the end: everything comes to an end when its 'ninety minutes' are up, and whether or not there is a cup-awarding ceremony will depend on what the individual believes about God.

In reality, belief systems are more complicated than this. A fundamental principle of Christian belief, as reiterated in the Christian creed, is that Christ 'will come again in glory to judge the living and the dead, and his kingdom will have no end': universal judgment will mark the beginning of eternal life (for those who are judged worthy of it) in God's kingdom. Where Christians differ is on the period leading up to that judgment.

The problem stems from different interpretations of the first few verses of Revelation 20, which recounts John's vision of the dragon, 'that ancient serpent, who is the Devil and Satan', being thrown into a pit, where he lies bound and enclosed for a thousand years. After that, says John, 'he must be loosed for a little while' (v. 3). While Satan languishes in his pit, martyred Christians are resurrected and reign with Christ for 1,000 years – a period which is sometimes referred to as Christ's 'millennial reign'. It is followed by the release of Satan, the judging of all the dead, and, eventually, the advent of the new heaven and new earth.

What are we waiting for? It depends which period of time Christians think we are currently living in. Is it the period before Christ reigns with his saints for 1,000 years? This is the belief of 'pre-millennialists' who have flourished particularly in the United States in the twentieth century. These believers anticipate Christ's return in bodily form and assume that the millennial reign will take place on earth (which is a likely interpretation of Revelation 20, since at the end of 1,000 years it is on earth that the forces of evil are once again unleashed).

The other belief, the view of 'post-millennialists', also sees this rule of Christ as taking place on earth, but holds that it has already started. We are living in the millennium now, and Jesus will return only at the end of the 1,000 years. In general, people who hold this view will be optimistic about the present, whereas pre-millennialists, particularly those in nineteenth- and twentieth-century America, see the present as a time of ever-increasing evil.

Either way of course a cataclysmic event looms large, whether it heralds the end of 1,000 years of peace which, for the post-millennialists, has begun almost imperceptibly, or whether it announces their beginning and Christ's return for the pre-millennialists. The difference between these approaches is significant when it comes to calculating the time of the end, because, as we shall see, it allows, if not a margin of error, then at least a certain flexibility in the arithmetic.

References

Augustine, *The City of God*, translated by Marcus Dods, introduction by Thomas Merton, 1950.

Henry Bettenson (editor and translator), *The Early Christian Fathers: A Selection from the Writings of the Fathers from St Clement of Rome to St Athanasius*, Oxford University Press, 1956.

G.B. Caird, *The Revelation of St John the Divine*, 2nd edition, A.&C. Black, London, 1984.

Henry Chadwick, *The Early Church*, Penguin Books, 1967.

J.E. Hurtgen, *Anti-language in the Apocalypse of John*, Edwin Mellen Press Ltd, Lampeter, 1993.

Gerd Theissen, *The Shadow of the Galilean: The Quest of the Historical Jesus in Narrative Form*, translated by John Bowden, SCM Press, 1987.

David Wenham, *The Rediscovery of Jesus' Eschatological Discourse*, Sheffield 1984.

Chapter 4

Signs of the End

*'As Jesus sat on the Mount of Olives, the disciples came
to him privately, saying "Tell us… what will be the sign
of your coming and of the close of the age?"'*

Matthew 24:3

Of all the popes in the early Christian centuries, I have a particular affection
for Pope Gregory I. 'Encouragement' might have been his middle name. At
the end of the sixth century it was Gregory who despatched Augustine to
preach Christianity to the English and who dealt kindly with him when a few
miles out of Rome Augustine and his companions got cold feet at having to
go to 'a barbarous, fierce and pagan nation, of whose very language they
were ignorant'. And Gregory did not confine his pastoral oversight to his
missionary bishops like Augustine. He wrote warmly and encouragingly to
the new converts, among them the Saxon King Ethelbert.

The letter from Gregory to Ethelbert in 601, as reproduced by Bede,
makes special mention of the expectation (based on Revelation 20:2-7) that
the world would end in the not-too-distant future:

We would also have Your Majesty know what we have learned from the
words of Almighty God in holy scripture, that the end of the present
world is at hand and the everlasting kingdom of the Saints is
approaching. When the end of the world is near, unprecedented things
occur – portents in the sky, terrors from heaven, unseasonable
tempests, wars, famines, pestilences, and widespread earthquakes. Not
all these things will happen during our own lifetimes, but will all ensue
in due course. Therefore, if any such things occur in your own country,
do not be anxious, for these portents of the end are sent to warn us to

consider the welfare of our souls and remember our last end, so that, when our Judge comes, He may find us prepared by good lives.

Gregory's reassuring tone may owe much to his own spiritual battle. According to one biographer, his conviction that the end was near caused him to confront his own anxiety; consequently his papacy was marked by 'solicitude' – anxious care for those for whom he had pastoral oversight. Even so, it is possible to discern in Gregory's reported words the essentially optimistic characteristic of mainline Christian belief. Christians who genuinely long for Christ's return can only welcome the signs of it, however terrifying these may appear. The teaching of Jesus had already offered the same reassurance: 'When you hear of wars and rumours of wars, do not be alarmed; this must take place, but the end is not yet' (Mark 13:7).

Popular preaching, though, and much of the art and literature which followed suit, adopted a less compassionate view. The signs of the end were meant to occasion terror, to inspire repentance through their fearfulness, which grew in intensity throughout the Middle Ages. The result is a marked shift in emphasis. The signs mentioned by Jesus and his followers cease to be seen as an encouragement, enabling Christians to concentrate ever more closely on preparing for the end itself. Instead they become a focus of interest in themselves, and a powerful weapon in the hands of those who prefer strong-arm tactics in getting their listeners to do as they are told. The signs of the end are used to terrorize the miserable sinner into the conviction of his own worthlessness; not to build him up, as Gregory might have wished, but to cast him down even further.

Using the threat of dreadful signs to terrify the sinful faithful is quite distinct from interpreting an apparent sign – where people look at anything from a comet in the sky or an eclipse of the sun to wars, moral disorder or natural disaster and say: this is it, the end is just around the corner. The urge to interpret – and the sects which have often been founded on it – would not have been possible if orthodox Christian teaching had not first set out and then elaborated the signs Christians believed would herald the end of the world and Christ's return.

Biblical signs

The biblical signs – and indeed those subsequently derived from them – point the way to chaos: a return to the primeval state at the time of creation, when 'the earth was without form and void, and darkness was upon the face of the deep' (Genesis 1:1). The wheel is seen to have turned full circle: the signs of the end threaten to plunge us back into the darkness whence we came.

The signs set out by Pope Gregory illustrate the two main categories in which such portents typically belong. There are the signs that happen wholly independently of human beings, which may take place either in the cosmos (portents in the skies and heavens) or in the natural world of our planet ('unseasonable' tempests and earthquakes). And there is the other category of signs which directly affect humankind, either because they are propagated by humans (wars) or experienced by them as events which have to do with the interaction of man and nature (famine and plague). The chaos to which these signs point is universal and inescapable: there is chaos in nature, in human affairs and in the relationship between the two.

This grouping can be found across the Old and New Testaments, though with differences in emphasis. In the Old Testament, the first chapter of the book of Joel is devoted to the detailed description of famine caused by a combination of locusts and drought, and its effect on human and animal life. This prophecy of what will precede the Day of the Lord probably reflects a good deal of contemporary human experience. Joel 2 then describes earthly and cosmic upheavals before the arrival of the Lord's army:

> The earth quakes before them
> > The heavens tremble,
> The sun and the moon are darkened,
> > and the stars withdraw their shining.

The only element missing is that of human conflicts, perhaps rendered unnecessary by the destruction famine has already brought to the people.

Jesus' description of signs preceding the end comes in Matthew 24:7, 29:

> Nation will rise against nation, and kingdom against kingdom, and there will be famines and earthquakes in various places... The sun will be darkened and the moon will not give its light, and the stars will fall from heaven, and the powers of the heavens will be shaken.

This is closely paralleled in Revelation 6, where the same events are depicted symbolically: the rider of the red horse is 'permitted to take peace from the earth, so that men should slay one another' (v. 4), food is sold at an impossibly high price, indicating famine ('a quart of wheat for a denarius', v. 6), the fourth rider kills with famine and pestilence (v. 8) and finally there is a dramatic description of the great earthquake, which goes far beyond anything else in Jewish or Christian writing to date – the cosmos itself is at an end:

> When he opened the sixth seal, I looked, and behold, there was a great earthquake; and the sun became black as sackcloth, the full moon became like blood, and the stars of the sky fell to the earth as the fig tree sheds its winter fruit when shaken by a gale; the sky vanished like a scroll that is rolled up, and every mountain and island was removed from its place (Revelation 6:12-14).

There is one particular sign of the end that sets Christian reflection apart from its Jewish contemporaries, and it has to do with persecution – the 'tribulation' of the saints, whose reception in heaven is described in Revelation 7. Unlike the signs of chaos, this is an ongoing process, and, like the increase in wickedness described below, it is not possible to point at a particular persecution and mark it out as the indication that the end has come. Nonetheless, Jesus' warning of this to his followers is recorded at length in all three synoptic gospels, and the theme of persecution before the end is taken up in the New Testament epistles, most notably in 2 Peter, 2 Thessalonians and 1 John. This theme is expressed through a further category of signs peculiar to Christian writing: Christians will know that the end is near when certain people appear whose function is to lead the faithful astray and to destroy their faith (though there is still a message of encouragement):

> Many false prophets will arise and lead many astray. And because wickedness is multiplied, most men's love will grow cold. But he who endures to the end will be saved (Matthew 24:11-13).

The appearance of false prophets, and ultimately Antichrist, who figures in 1 and 2 John and is alluded to in 2 Thessalonians 2, is a specifically Christian sign of the end, and we shall consider them separately (as 'People of the End') in due course.

It is not hard to see why these different signs have exercised such a fascination over the centuries. Their potential for gripping the imagination is immense and is reflected in art and literature, while their power to terrify is greater still. They strike at everything to which we owe our existence: food and light, health, climate, and freedom from personal attack. Little wonder, then, that they figure not just as warnings of disaster ahead. Anyone who claims to identify an event in nature or human affairs with one of these signs is able to exercise very great power over those who believe him. But as for the signs themselves, how have they developed since Jesus took the traditonal Jewish signs of the end and added to them the persecution of his own followers?

Intertestamental literature

The signs of the end mentioned in the books of the Old Testament had been around for a few centuries by the time of Jesus. It is clear from the gospels that by the time of Jesus' birth, many Jews were actively anticipating the arrival of their Messiah – a leader who would bring about the Day of the Lord – at virtually any moment. We have already seen how this expectation is reflected in Jewish writing both before and after the time of Christ in the writings of the centuries known as 'intertestamental', roughly from the second century BC to the second century AD, and with it went some development in the expression of ideas about the end. It is important to remember that the 'canons' – or authoritative contents list – of the Old and New Testaments were not settled until a relatively late date: at the Jewish synod of Jamnia in AD90 for the Old Testament (although the list of prophetic books had been finalized by the third century BC) and the late fourth century AD for the New. People were reading other writings inspired by Christian or Jewish belief during this time and indeed did not cease to do so once the canons were fixed. The rejected books continued to be read and valued and to exert their influence. And the later popular formulations of signs of the end owe as much to some of these texts as they do to the canonical scriptures.

2 Esdras (4 Ezra)

The Old Testament Apocrypha (regarded by the Roman Catholic Church as part of the Old Testament canon) contains just one book which qualifies as an example of apocalyptic writing: 2 Esdras, which is sometimes referred to also as 4 Ezra. The bulk of 2 Esdras (chapters 3 to 14) was probably written by a Palestinian Jew in the late first century AD, and in it the archangel Uriel reveals mysteries about the end to the prophet Ezra in a series of seven visions. His description of the signs occupies much of chapters 5 and 6; it is not only more detailed than anything in the other scriptures, but there are more signs of the chaos to come.

One thing I have learnt from reading 2 Esdras, and books like it, is that it is really not possible to categorize chaos after all. In this book the neat categories I suggested earlier to describe the biblical signs of the end are themselves jumbled up in just a couple of verses: chaos in the cosmos is intermingled with chaos in nature, which takes on human properties. The world is truly turned upside down, as the English Puritan writers were later to appreciate:

> If the Most High grants that you live, you shall see [the land]
> thrown into confusion...
> and the sun shall suddenly shine forth at night,
> and the moon during the day.
> Blood shall drip from wood,
> and the stone shall utter its voice;
> the peoples shall be troubled and the stars shall fall
> (2 Esdras 5:4-5).

In the human sphere, chaos does not simply result from people turning against one another: it invades their very being: 'menstrous women shall bring forth monsters' (5:8). The patterns of normal existence are swept aside: 'Infants a year old shall speak with their voices, and women with child shall give birth to premature children at three or four months, and these shall live and dance' (6:21). Such portents are directly echoed in accounts of unnatural births in later centuries and taken to be signs of the end.

The natural world is turned upside down just as much as the human one, and again this is a theme taken up by medieval and post-medieval writers. Particularly, though, the signs reflect the probably well-founded belief that animals and birds are peculiarly sensitive to changes in the atmosphere. In 2 Esdras 5 the prophet is told that 'the birds shall fly away together; and the sea of Sodom shall cast up fish... wild animals shall roam beyond their haunts' (vv. 6, 7, 8).

The world of nature is also affected by events taking place among humans (whereas in Joel, for example, the reverse is true):

> At that time friends shall make war on friends like enemies, and the earth and those who inhabit it shall be terrified, and the springs of the fountains shall stand still, so that for three hours they shall not flow (6:24).

The parallel with the darkness that descended on the earth for three hours at the time of Christ's crucifixion is unmistakable.

None of this is restricted to religious writing of the intertestamental period. Secular literature before and since portrays nature as both reflecting human events and as issuing a warning of what is to come. In the *Georgics*, written two or three decades before the birth of Christ, Virgil uses the sun in this dual role:

> Who dares call the sun a liar?
> Often too he warns you of lurking imminent violence,
> Of treachery, and wars that grow in the dark like a cancer.
> The sun, when Caesar fell, had sympathy for Rome –
> That day he hid the brightness of his head in a rusty fog
> And an evil age was afraid his night would last for ever
> (Book I, 463-68).

The evil of forthcoming civil war is signalled by the behaviour of animals, an eruption of Mount Etna ('rolling up great balls of flame and molten rocks'), thunder and lightning, as well as more sinister events:

> Likewise in stilly woods a voice was heard by many –
> A monster voice, and phantoms miraculously pale
> Were met at the dusk of night, and cattle spoke – an omen
> Unspeakable! Rivers stopped, earth gaped, and ivories
> In temples wept sad tears...
> Never elsewhere have lightnings flickered so constantly
> In a clear sky, or baleful comets burned so often
> (476-80, 487-88).

The background to the end-time is an increase in human wickedness (see Matthew 24:12). As already suggested, this is a cumulative process rather than a one-off dramatic event. Many people have looked at their own times and thought that things could not get any worse – that the end must be very near. But the problem is that since there is said to be a progression in wickedness it is virtually impossible to tell when that process is complete. As a sign it is more like a constant background to the other signs we have considered. The writer of 2 Esdras puts it like this: 'Then shall reason hide itself, and wisdom shall withdraw into its chamber, and it shall be sought by many but shall not be found, and unrighteousness shall increase on earth' (5:9-10). Human disorder is not just a matter of outright war: there will be 'tumult of peoples, intrigues of nations, wavering of leaders, confusion of princes' (9:3). However, there is ultimately a message of hope for those who remain after all these events:

> And it shall be that whoever remains after all that I have foretold you shall himself be saved and shall see my salvation and the end of my world. And they shall see the men who were taken up, who from their birth have not tasted death; and the heart of the earth's inhabitants shall be changed and converted to a different spirit. For evil shall be blotted out and deceit shall be quenched; faithfulness shall flourish, and corruption shall be overcome, and the truth, which has been so long without fruit, shall be revealed (6:25-28).

For all the disorder in the account of chaos, there emerges a logic in the writing of 2 Esdras. Chapter 6:38-55 recalls the days of creation with the implication that each element of creation will be thrown into turmoil before the end. The angel's account of what will follow all the signs of the end makes this clear: 'The world shall be turned back to primeval silence for seven days, as it was at the first beginnings.' Once again, the wheel seems to have come full circle.

1 Enoch

The first book of Enoch, with its 108 chapters, is a giant among Jewish texts. For the first three Christian centuries it was regarded by at least some authorities in the West as part of the Old Testament canon (and is quoted with approval in the New Testament letter of Jude), while in the East its popularity continued until the ninth century. It is probably a collection of five books, of which the fourth book, sometimes called the Book of Dreams (chs 83–90) is of interest here. Except for the first couple of chapters, this consists of what is often referred to as the 'animal apocalypse'.

The curious thing about this is that the events of the end are projected back in time to the days of Adam. Chapters 85 onward are essentially a description of the history of the world using terms rich in symbolism and apocalyptic imagery. Enoch (who was the father of Methuselah) describes his vision to his son in surreal terms: Adam is depicted as a bull rising out of the earth; he and his descendants are attacked by stars dropping from heaven (a reference to the fallen angels of Genesis 6:4), who in at least one version change into bulls themselves. From the union of the 'star' bulls from heaven and those from the earth are born elephants, camels and asses: general mayhem ensues and 'all the children of the earth began to tremble and shake before them, and to flee' (86:6). This is only the beginning of a tale of destruction involving large animals and birds of prey who attack sheep, symbols of purity. When Enoch awakes the sheep have been secured within a house by 'the Lord of the sheep', and judgment pronounced on the wicked shepherds. Eventually the wheel comes full circle: a single huge white bull is born, and all other species are transformed into white bulls themselves – a symbol of a new Eden. But Enoch can only weep at the certainty of the chaos that is to come: 'My tears... ran down on account of that which I saw, for everything will come to pass and be fulfilled; and all the deeds of men in their order were shown to me' (90:39).

Familiar elements are put to unfamiliar use: the stars dropping from heaven as a sign of the end are related to a specific incident in Israel's history; the chaos among animals becomes a metaphor for past warfare, while individual animals represent human beings both in the past and in the future, as indeed they do in the book of Daniel, where the ram and the goat in Daniel 8 represent the empires of Persia and Greece.

The sign of fire

Fire is a particularly potent symbol. As a natural sign it is linked with other indications of doom: flashing lightning, an erupting volcano. But fire is also an all-pervasive religious or mythological element. In Zoroastrianism it is venerated as the life-giving force that purifies the world of evil. In the Jewish scriptures it is symbolic of the power of God: God speaks to Moses out of the fire (Deuteronomy 4:12) and is himself described as 'a devouring fire' (Deuteronomy 4:24). Fire represents the all-powerful word of God in Jeremiah: 'Is not my word like fire... and like a hammer which breaks the rock in pieces?' (Jeremiah 23:29), while the Holy Spirit of God in the New Testament appears as 'tongues of fire' to the disciples at Pentecost (Acts 2).

When fire is included among the signs of the end, it inevitably has wider connotations than might at first appear, and believers cannot fail to take it seriously. Consequently, in apocalyptic writing, fire is not just a sign but a specific calamity of the end: it burns up the earth. The multiple meanings are combined in 2 Esdras 16:

> The Lord God sends calamities, and who will drive them away? Fire will go forth from his wrath, and who is there to quench it? He will flash lightning, and who will not be afraid? He will thunder, and who will not be terrified?... Behold, calamities are sent forth and shall not return until they come over the earth. The fire is kindled, and shall not be put out until it consumes the foundations of the earth (2 Esdras 16:8-10, 14-15).

The writer of 2 Peter takes up this idea and combines it with Jesus' teaching that the end will come – 'like a thief in the night' – when people least expect it:

> The day of the Lord will come like a thief, and then the heavens will pass away with a loud noise, and the elements will be dissolved with fire, and the earth and the works that are upon it will be burned up (2 Peter 3:10).

The thirteenth-century English 'Doomsday' poem reflects this tradition. Consuming fire is put as the final stage before the end:

> That fire shall come in this world one Saturday night
> Burning all this world as Christ it will ordain.

Nonetheless, the most familiar connotation of fire nowadays is probably the fire of hell. This too has an ancient history, taking up the association made in the Ancient Near East between fire and judgment, which is epitomized in God's punishment of the cities of Sodom and Gomorrah with fire and brimstone (Genesis 19:24). The image of fire being used not just to purify but to test for value (as a refiner tests gold with fire) occurs often in the New Testament. The apostle Paul makes the connection between the fire that tests and judgment at the end:

Each man's work will become manifest, for the Day will disclose it, because it will be revealed with fire, and the fire will test what sort of work each one has done (1 Corinthians 3:13).

In *The Testament of Abraham*, a work probably of Jewish origin which enjoyed great popularity in the first few centuries of the Christian church, fire is associated with recording angels: two angels stand alongside God, the one on his right recording good deeds, the one on the left, bad. The right-hand angel, Dokiel, holds an honestly balanced pair of scales as he weighs good and bad deeds, and dispenses divine justice. The other angel is the Archangel Pyruel, who

...has power over fire and tests man's deeds by fire. If the fire burns up a man's deed, the angel of judgment takes him at once and carries him off to a sinner's place – a most disagreeable place of punishment. If the fire tests a man's deed and does not touch it, he is accounted righteous... So... all things in all men are tested by fire and scales (*Testament of Abraham*, XIII, 17-20).

The imagery of fire is complex. As new meanings are added to existing ones, it is not hard to imagine how terrifying the idea of fire as a sign of the end must have become to ordinary people, who would already have seen it as the most awe-inspiring of natural phenomena. And it is an imagery that has gripped the imagination of artists down the centuries.

Signs in history

The signs I have been looking at so far have all been used as portents: they will all appear at some time in the future. For the early Christians this was important to know, not just because they were wondering how soon the end would come, but because they wanted to be sure they had not missed anything. The idea that Jesus might somehow return without people realizing it was too awful to contemplate and this concern is reflected in 2 Thessalonians. The writer, who was more likely a follower of Paul than Paul himself, says, 'We beg you... not to be quickly shaken in mind or excited, either by spirit or by word, or by letter purporting to be from us, to the effect that the day of the Lord has come' (2 Thessalonians 2:1-2), and he goes on to detail various events that must precede Christ's coming that will be unmistakable.

Yet as the years and centuries pass, the signs of the end undergo a shift in reference: they are used not only in predictions of what will happen in the future, but also to make sense of the present. The presence of such signs must mean that the end is near. This brings a certain comfort, at least to the faithful, when people are confronted with events that make their lives wretched and which are beyond their control – such as wars, plagues and famines. And it offers some explanation for the inexplicable, like the meteor shower observed in AD763, the procession of comets and eclipses in the heavens and the bizarre human and animal behaviour on earth, which brought a sense of helplessness and terror to our medieval forefathers. In the turbulent years leading up to the French Revolution, and in the wake of an outbreak of sunspots in 1777, the 1780s were marked by unusually severe weather. This, and the appearance of a number of novels on the subject of the end of the world, suggest a desire to try to impose some sort of logic on the social disorders of the time.

A further factor comes into play when signs are actively sought in order to confirm certain beliefs. This typically happens when an individual or a community is convinced that the world will end on a certain date. Any unusual happening in the period leading up to that time – the appearance of a comet, or some kind of human disaster, say – is interpreted as a sign of the end and so gives added support to the date in question, as we shall see in due course.

Events which have been seen as signs that the end is near for either of these last two reasons are many and varied. But they are all recognizable developments of the signs described in early Judeo-Christian writing, as are beliefs centred on individuals, which will be the focus of chapter 5. Undoubtedly many of the stories have improved with the telling, but behind them lie genuine events in history. Usually such events take on a wholly undeserved significance by virtue of the belief in the end-time which people have projected onto them.

This is particularly true where popular belief has developed some of the less conventional signs mentioned in intertestamental sources. If there is no immediate connection to be made with other signs or with a date in the near future when the end is expected, then they are treated as dreadful warnings of what might come to pass. One such case in the seventeenth century has to do with birds, whose behaviour is always of interest in folklore, even if it is only to predict the weather. In 2 Esdras 5:6 birds are sensitive to impending disaster ('And one shall reign whom those who dwell on earth do not expect, and birds shall fly away together') and several instances of unpredictable bird behaviour are recounted in seventeenth-century popular ballads. These were the equivalent of our tabloid newspapers, and did not aspire to being art or poetry. They often focus on the strange or sensational, and, like their modern counterparts, may adopt a strong moralizing tone.

One day in 1621 two flights of starlings converged from opposite directions above the Irish city of Cork. The exact date is uncertain: some sources suggest it was in May, others put it in September or October of the same year. Either way, with hindsight, the event was seen as an evil portent, since the city itself was devastated by a fire caused by lightning, the following year, at the end of May 1622. All these events are described in several ballads, each called 'The Battle of the Birds', which are spiced up with calls to repentance. In portraying the darkness, thunder and lightning of the 1622 events, the writer reminds his readers of the previous year's events:

> As at the East the Stares [starlings] began their Fight
> And there fell downe the Birds first, kild outright.
> So at the East began the Fire to flame,
> Those at the West did soone beholde the same.

The second part of the 25-stanza poem consists of eleven verses urging people to repent:

> If men Repentance in this life doe stay
> Let them consider of the Judgment day:
> When God to sinners shall say in his Ire,
> Goe hence yee Cursed to Eternall Fire.

This was no isolated event. Fifty years later, in France, a 'battle of the birds' is recorded on 26 February 1676 above the area between Dole and Sulines. There are many different types of birds and they are seen as a punishment for people's sins. The outcome of the battle is unpleasant:

> Five hundred paces, as 'tis said,
> Of ground were covered with the dead,
> Unto the height of any man,
> besides some thousands scattered.

But in this case the writer has no event to which to link this portent – the birds are just a horrible warning:

> What is the meaning of the same,
> there's none doth know but God above.
> Then let us fear his holy name,
> and live in concord, peace and love.

Portents associated with the end of the world are commonly transferred to the death of outstanding human beings, when events are viewed in retrospect. The ninth-century account of the life of Charlemagne by Einhard the Frank described the signs which marked the approach of the emperor's death. In the last three years of Charles' life, he writes, 'there occurred repeatedly eclipses of both the sun and the moon; and a black-coloured spot was to be seen on the sun for seven days at a stretch.' These natural portents were reinforced by more earthly happenings, which were insignificant on their own, but acquire importance later on: the portico between Charles' palace and the cathedral crashed down, and a wooden bridge across the Rhine caught fire. On Charles' last expedition to Saxony to fight the King of the Danes a meteor flashed across the sky from right to left, there were earth tremors at Aachen, and the cathedral was struck by lightning. A golden apple on the highest point of the roof was 'dashed off by a thunderbolt' and thrown onto the Bishop's house next door. Charles took no notice at the time, not believing that all this had anything to do with him. His biographer, with hindsight, knew better.

Some events are so horrendous as to signal the end of the world by themselves. Some of the great wars and plagues in history are cases in point. Seen as signs of God's judgment on sinful humanity, they are quickly associated in people's minds with other, less immediately devastating signs of the end.

Philip Ziegler has described how the Black Death, a series of plague epidemics felt particularly severely in England in 1348, was met with resignation by an uncomprehending population: 'If the plague was decreed by God and the inexorable movement of the planets, how could frail man seek to oppose it?' Ziegler quotes Archbishop Zouche of York, who warned his congregations that the plague must be 'caused by the sins of men who, made complacent by their prosperity, forget the bounty of the most high Giver'. In that year the city of Hull was flooded by the river Humber; a few miles to the north there was an earthquake on the Friday before Passion Sunday; and Siamese twins were born and died at Kingston-upon-Hull. On New Year's Eve the Ouse flooded at York. Set against the background of the plague's relentless progression north, these events took on new and sinister meaning.

Well before the plague finally disappeared, political turmoil added to the upheaval in the form of the Peasants' Revolt of 1381, which was followed the next year by an earthquake. An anonymous poet has recorded in an eleven-stanza poem entitled 'Verses on the Earthquake of 1382', how these events were to be regarded as portents of the end:

> The rysing of the comuynes in Londe
> the Pestilens and the eorthe-quake –
> These three things I understonde
> Beo-tokenes the grete vengaunce and wrake
> That shulde falle for synnes sake…
> ('The peasants' uprising, the plague and the earthquake betoken
> the great vengeance and wrath to come because of sin.')

Each verse ends with the idea that these events are a warning. Yet the poem ends on a hopeful note, since there is still time to repent:

> And thanke that child that Marie bare,
> Of his gret godnesse and his gras,
> Sende us such warnyng to beware.
> ('Thank the child whom Mary bore, that of his great goodness
> and grace he should send us such a warning to be alert.')

The fourteenth and fifteenth centuries were obsessed with death – as pictures of the 'dance of death' illustrate all too clearly, with the skeletal figure of death breathing down the necks of aristocrats and peasants alike. But similar combinations of events continued to trigger thoughts of the end – witness Defoe's *Journal of the Plague Year* published in 1722. Today this might be called 'faction' – a fictionalized account of the plague which swept London in 1665, presented as a warning of the renewed dangers of the plague which in 1720 had come as close as Marseille. It purports to be genuine history and makes extensive reference to verifiable events. Foremost among these is the appearance of comets over London, which are also mentioned in Pepys' diaries for December 1664 and April 1665. (There is, of course, nothing new in comets being taken as ill omens, as the appearance of Halley's comet in 1066 testifies.) Defoe refers to the popular belief that 'those two Comets pass'd directly over the City, and that so very near the Houses, that it was plain, they imported something peculiar to the City alone.' He goes on, 'These Things had a more than ordinary Influence upon the Minds of the common People, and they had almost universal mellancholly Apprehensions of some dreadful Calamity and Judgment coming upon the City.' Things were made worse by astrologers and prophets who roamed the streets preaching destruction. As the plague raged, Defoe's narrator comments that its effect was to bring Dissenters back to the parish churches – a unity that lasted only as long as the epidemic itself.

Throughout the Middle Ages and beyond, the various signs of the end exerted an almost tyrannical hold over the minds of ordinary people. It would be tempting to surmise that scientific advances and the advent of rationalism did away with all that, but this was far from being the case. At one level there is a certain truth in it – following Pierre Bayle, it came to be recognized by scientists and educated people that comets were natural phenomena and did not signify disaster (though given the catastrophic consequences which we now know would follow a collision between natural phenomena such as meteorites and our planet, our forebears were perhaps wise to be fearful). By the seventeenth century it was claimed that only strictly biblical prophecies were taken seriously and not always these. Peter Burke quotes the case of the Yorkshire minister who was asked by his congregation not to bother with the topic of the millennium which was 'not a profitable subject'.

Yet whatever the educated classes may have understood, belief in signs of the end continued to flourish among the ordinary folk. Popular ballads of the sixteenth century describe unnatural births and deformities which point to chaos in the natural order. The idea that everything is in decline remains popular; according to a seventeenth-century almanac,

The world itself is dying and decaying,
The earth more sensible, heavenly stars more straying.

Paradoxically, science itself could make its contribution to the signs of the end, as astrology had done before it. The discovery of a new star in 1572 was taken to be the sign of Christ's Second Coming. Natural events such as the Lisbon earthquake of 1755 and political upheavals such as the English

Civil War and the French Revolution were all good sources for those searching for signs of the end. But those who sought to match biblical signs with events taking place around them in the first 1900 years of Christianity seem almost orthodox in their outlook in comparison with some of the frankly bizarre couplings of signs and events that have emerged in the course of the twentieth century, as we shall see in chapter 9.

The New Testament writers are emphatic that the faithful must not be led astray by the 'signs and wonders' they will undoubtedly encounter: 'False Christs and false prophets will arise and show signs and wonders, to lead astray, if possible, the elect,' says Jesus in Mark 13:22. What, then, are Christians to make of those apparent signs which so closely resemble what they believe will happen at the end? The church has not been above manipulating extraordinary events in both the natural world and human activity for its own ends. To support their cause, the historians of the Crusades were 'particularly alert for miracles', says Benedicta Ward. Once such 'signs' are placed within the framework of history, they can be used for virtually anything: 'The detection of the hand of God in political events was set within a wider view of history itself as propaganda, in which the rise and fall of nations were signs from God to men.'

Islam

It is said that when the Caliph Umar entered Jerusalem in 638 the patriarch declared this to be the 'abomination of desolation'. It is ironic, then, that Islam, the religion of the so-called infidel, should have much in common with both Judaism and Christianity in its understanding of signs presaging and revealing God's activities.

The Koran, like the Jewish Bible, presents God as revealed through his creation. Like some of Jesus' parables in the New Testament, it portrays unbelievers as ignoring God's warning to be prepared for the Day of Judgment. In the Koran God speaks too of a new creation: 'On that day We shall roll up the heaven like a scroll of parchment. Just as We brought the First Creation into being, so will We restore it. This is a promise We shall assuredly fulfil' (21:105).

The signs of this approaching end are also couched in fairly familiar terms: 'The hour of Doom is drawing near, and the moon is cleft in two. Yet, when they see a sign, the unbelievers turn their backs and say "Ingenious sorcery!'" (54:1). There is to be a separation of the damned and the righteous, heralded by the destruction of the earth: 'When the earth shakes and quivers, and the mountains crumble away and scatter abroad into fine dust, you shall be divided...' (56:6). The end of time is called 'The Cessation' and it is characterized by the natural world turned upside down, with some characteristically Eastern details:

> When the sun ceases to shine; when the stars fall down and the mountains are blown away; when camels big with young are left untended, and the wild beasts are brought together; when the seas are set alight... then each soul shall know what it has done (81:1).

Similar cosmic disorder before the end marks the section entitled 'The Cataclysm':

> When the sky is rent asunder; when the stars scatter and the oceans roll together; when the graves are hurled about; each soul shall know what it has done and what it has failed to do (82:1).

The twelfth-century theologian Abu Hamid al-Ghazali also lamented the failure of the faithful to take seriously the inevitability of the day of judgment and its implications for human behaviour in this life. 'Beware denying any of the wonders of the Day because they fail to accord with the measure of mundane things,' he warned in his *Revival of the Religious Sciences*. His description of the last day of earthly time is particularly interesting in that the apocalyptic signs which precede it include the reversal of the natural order – the sun rises in the west – and the overturning of the moral order – pride prevails over piety.

The signs of the end are perhaps the most constant elements in the whole tradition. They are typically phenomena that remain beyond the power of ordinary mortals to control (such as the weather and movement of heavenly bodies) or those which perhaps they fear (chaos in the moral and social order). Yet many of the descriptions of these portents of disaster to come have a curiously poetic quality about them, that perhaps is inherent in the whole subject. That impression was reinforced when I read a short essay by a thirteen-year-old schoolgirl on how she imagined the end of the world. Lorna Powner could have had little, if any, exposure to the traditions I have outlined in this chapter. She wrote:

I think that one day unexpected, the skies will cloud over with thick, jet-black clouds that no one has ever witnessed in their whole lives before. Darkness will haunt every place over the globe and people will soon realize, with a trembling fear, that the end of the world has come. All the trees and plants of any kind will fade mysteriously and wither to the crusty ground. Animals, large and small, will flee for miles, but they will never escape the choking darkness. Soon a wind, a cool soft wind, will sweep across the earth halting all movement, children stop crying and animals pause in their tracks. All living things watch the sky with a solemn glare, then small sparks flash in the sky with a distant bang. The stars are heating up and exploding, millions of them covering the dark skies then just disappearing. Suddenly the moon slips from sight and with a huge deafening BANG the sun ends its long, long life and is never to be seen again. The earth starts to spin rapidly then shoots off into the universe leaving people's souls rising up to heaven. This is how I imagine it!

References

Bede, *A History of the English Church and People*, 731, translated by L. Sherley-Price; revised edition 1968, Harmondsworth, Penguin.

Carleton Brown (editor), *Lyrics of the Fourteenth Century*, Oxford University Press, 1924.

Carleton Brown (editor), *Lyrics of the Thirteenth Century*, Oxford University Press, 1932.

Peter Burke, *Popular Culture in Early Medieval Europe*, London, Temple Smith, 1978.

B.S. Capp, *English Almanacs, 1500–1800*, New York, Ithaca, 1979.

Daniel Defoe, *A Journal of the Plague Year*, edited by Louis Landa, Oxford University Press, 1969.

Einhard, *Vita Caroli*, in *Two Lives of Charlemagne*, translated by Lewis Thorpe, Penguin Books, 1969.

H.E. Rollins (editor), *A Pepysian Garland: Black-letter broadside ballads 1595–1639*, Harvard University Press, 1971.

Carol Straw, *Gregory the Great: Perfection in Imperfection*, University of California Press, Berkeley, London, 1988.

Virgil, *Georgics*, translated by C. Day Lewis, Oxford University Press, 1966.

David Waines, *An Introduction to Islam*, Cambridge University Press, 1995.

Benedicta Ward, *Miracles and the Medieval Mind: Theory, Record and Event, 1000–1215*, London: Scolar Press, 1982.

Philip Ziegler, *The Black Death*, 1969; Penguin Books, 1982.

Chapter 5

People of the End

'Children, it is the last hour; and as you have heard that antichrist is coming, so now many antichrists have come; therefore we know that it is the last hour.'

1 John 2:18

The rich variety of signs and events which from ancient times have been believed to herald the end of the world is not quite the whole story. There are also some people in the end-time scenario. And unlike any number of prophets who have claimed that the end is imminent, these figures are integral to the unfolding of the whole drama.

Already in Zoroastrianism specific figures were identified: the books of the Middle Persian period state that the end would be marked by the appearance of three 'helpers' (Saoshyants) who would be born of virgins, and known as 'sons of Zarathustra'. With Christianity there arose at least three major traditions relating to various people who were expected to emerge just before the end. The traditions grew up unevenly, so there is no neat succession or order to the way in which these people appear. But they are all individuals who, it is assumed, will be recognized for who and what they are.

Insofar as these figures are distinctive, they are clearly separate from the false prophets promised by Jesus in Matthew 24, who are signs of the end rather than people of it. They are also different in that they are no ordinary human beings. They may be heroic figures from a nation's past, whether real or legendary, who return after a long period in which they were 'asleep' somewhere on earth. They may be figures from a religious past – prophets who return to earth from heaven. Or they may be people of the future, such as Antichrist – a supernatural figure who takes human form, and whose family history and activities are a perverse reflection of those of the true Christ, with the function above all of deceiving and misleading the faithful.

In this case Antichrist is sometimes opposed by a human hero: a pope or emperor of the future.

Traditions like these, which are attached to real people or at least to supernatural figures in human form, have provoked the same abundance of interpretations as the various signs of the end. This is at least partly because traditions relating to people and signs can both be used to make sense of unusual or disturbing events. With signs it might work like this. Besides saying 'I know that the world will end and when the moon disappears in an eclipse I believe that it will happen very soon,' people might also think along these lines: 'I am upset and confused by the disappearing moon. But if the world is about to end, then I understand why it has turned black.' When there are particular human or supernatural figures associated with the end, there is a similar statement of belief: 'I know that before the end comes the world will see the return of certain prophets and the appearance of Antichrist.' But if the circumstances appear to warrant it, this can easily be reformulated: 'This person is evil: I will call him Antichrist, and now I understand why he's so evil. The end must be near.'

'Since the Middle Ages,' writes R.K. Emmerson, 'interpretations of Antichrist... have been manipulated to attack religious institutions and political opponents.' In other words, the expectation that certain signs and certain people will precede the end allows people to make their own identifications. A religious or political group can manipulate its members by claiming that the wickedness of the opposition is that of Antichrist himself; or that the perfection of a national hero points to a special role for him (and, by implication, for his people) at the end of time. In this way secular history – people and events – is given eschatological significance. It is relatively easy to dismiss passing comets, earthquakes or plagues as events which took on eschatological overtones in the over-active imagination of just a few people. But identifying specific people as precursors of the end has a much wider influence, and may find a place in the folklore of an entire nation. The traditions of certain people emerging immediately prior to the end of time are virtually inseparable from the ways in which those traditions have been interpreted – the identifications that have been imposed on them.

The Two Witnesses

I will grant my Two Witnesses power to prophesy for one thousand two hundred and sixty days, clothed in sackcloth (Revelation 11:3).

There are two characters in the Old Testament who do not die but are taken directly up into heaven, and in Christian tradition they soon came to be identified with the witnesses in Revelation 11. The first is Enoch, who makes only a brief appearance in Genesis 5 as one of the godly men who lived before the flood. He is received into God's presence (Genesis 5:25) at the comparatively young age, but possibly a significant one, of 365 years (his son Methuselah lived until he was 969).

Like the later Christian writer to the Hebrews, the author of the Wisdom of Solomon portrays Enoch as an outstanding example of a righteous man, and attributes his assumption into heaven to God's desire to keep him that way:

> There was one who pleased God and was loved by him,
> and while living among sinners he was taken up.
> He was caught up lest evil change his undertanding
> or guile deceive his soul (Wisdom 5, 10-11).

The book of Sirach (Ecclesiasticus) also sees him as an example. Enoch is included in the list of famous men (chapter 44), as one who 'pleased the Lord, and was taken up; he was an example of repentance to all generations' (44:16). In addition, the wisdom tradition of the intertestamental period portrays Enoch as outstanding for his scientific knowledge:

> He was the first among men born on earth to learn to write and to acquire knowledge and wisdom; and he wrote down in a book details about the signs of heaven according to the order of their months...
> And he was the first to write a testimony; and he warned the sons of men about what would happen in future generations on the earth...
> And what was and what will be he saw in a vision in his sleep, just as it will happen to the sons of men in every generation till the day of judgment (Jubilees 4:17, 18, 19).

This is reflected in chapters 72 to 82 of 1 Enoch, which constitute 'the book of the revolutions of the lights of heaven' revealed to Enoch by the archangel Uriel. Again according to Jubilees, Enoch's righteousness and wisdom earned him a special position in world history:

> In his life on earth Noah surpassed all mortal men in achieving perfect righteousness, except Enoch; for Enoch had a special function to be a

witness to the world's generations and report all the deeds of each generation till the day of judgment (Jubilees 10:17).

Enoch also appears as the culmination of yet another tradition, that of the appearance of the Son of Man from Daniel 7:13. In 1 Enoch 71 the writer describes how his spirit was taken into heaven to be greeted by the angels and archangels, including one who says: 'You are the Son of Man who was born to righteousness, and righteousness remains over you, and the righteousness of the Head of Days will not leave you... There will be length of days with that Son of Man, and the righteous will have peace...' (14, 17). Earlier in the same book, though, the Son of man is seen as an angelic being with no previous existence (1 Enoch 48) and the passage in chapter 71 is probably a later, possibly even Christian, addition. Nonetheless, it is a clear indication of the popularity of Enoch and the significant claims made for him in the intertestamental period.

It is widely assumed that these claims had their origin among the Jews in Babylon and the East, since there is some evidence of Babylonian influence on the legend. Like the magi from the East in the gospel narratives, Enoch is credited with comprehensive knowledge of the stars and their movements; and the description of the punishment of fallen angels in 1 Enoch 67 is strongly reminiscent of Zoroastrian teaching on the ordeal by molten metal.

In spite of the widespread interest in Enoch at the time when the Book of Revelation was written, it is by no means the case that interpreters agree that he is one of the Two Witnesses mentioned in chapter 11. Perhaps this is because he holds less interest for Christian writers who are not party to the long-standing Jewish tradition about him. The same cannot be said for the other likely witness.

The tradition that the prophet Elijah will return in the last days is one which pervades Christian writings and belief on the end-times throughout history. This is probably because Elijah, together with Moses, appears with Christ at his Transfiguration (Mark 9:4) and in the conversation between Jesus and his disciples which follows, Jesus does not deny that 'Elijah does come first to restore all things' (Mark 9:12). In this context, though, Jesus seems to be identifying John the Baptist as fulfilling the role of Elijah.

Elijah was taken into heaven in rather more spectacular manner than Enoch – caught up in a whirlwind with a chariot and horses of fire (2 Kings 2:11). The belief that the great prophet of Israel would return is expressed most fully in the Old Testament in the concluding verses of Malachi, which may have been intended to wind up the whole collection of books of the so-called minor prophets:

> Behold I will send you Elijah the prophet before the great and terrible day of the Lord comes. And he will turn the hearts of fathers to their children and the hearts of children to their fathers, lest I come and smite the land with a curse (Malachi 4:5-6).

This role of Elijah as peacemaker and, particularly, as restorer of Israel is singled out by the writer of Ecclesiasticus who, in his recital of famous men, describes Elijah as 'ready at the appointed time... to calm the wrath of God before it breaks out in fury, to turn the heart of the father to the son, and to restore the tribes of Jacob' (48:10). Elsewhere Elijah has other functions: anointing the Messiah or awakening the dead on judgment day.

Both Elijah and Enoch may be seen as Christ-like in that their respective departures from earth prefigure Christ's ascension. In the earliest Christian tradition it is Elijah alone who is to return, although within a couple of centuries this has been largely replaced by the idea of two witnesses. (Later, however, the Franciscan order was to claim that St Francis was Elijah, and that the Two Witnesses would be Franciscan monks.) Their function at the end-time is to confront Antichrist and reconvert the Christians whom he has led astray. In some versions they are killed, only to return to life three and a half days later and to rejoin the saints in heaven. Some sources see their task as specifically to convert the Jews – who may first have become followers of Antichrist.

With the Reformation and its attacks on medieval scholasticism, belief in the literal return of Enoch and Elijah began to disappear. As Emmerson puts it: 'Most Protestant exegetes emphasize that the "spirit" of Elias was present in John the Baptist (Matthew 11:14), that the same "spirit" is now present in the last days in the teaching of scripture, and that it is dangerous to expect the physical return of Enoch and Elias.' However, this meant that the way was now wide open for identifying the Two Witnesses not with biblical characters but with contemporary individuals.

The Muggletonians

In 1636 two London weavers proclaimed themselves to be the last witnesses of Revelation 11. However, the better known seventeenth-century claimants to the title emerged early in the 1650s: they were Ludowick Muggleton and John Reeve.

The timing has to be significant. The execution of Charles I in 1649 has been hailed as a triumph for the Puritans, yet the country as a whole was uneasy at what had been done, and the English republicans met with a cold reception in the outside world. The church had lost its leader as well as its monarch, bishops had been abolished, and independent sects were springing up everywhere, most of them firmly opposed to any form of church discipline. It was very much in keeping with the millennial atmosphere of the 1640s that on Charles' death many people felt that the anointed king could be followed only by Christ himself.

It is hardly surprising, then, that a number of the new sects were particularly interested in the end-time. Muggleton and Reeve were the founders of the Muggletonians, a radical sect which was noted for its hostility to church order of any kind and to intellectuals, and which survived until the twentieth century. In a book published in 1665, Muggleton described himself as one of 'the Two last commissionated [sic] Witnesses and Prophets of the only high, immortal, glorious God, Christ Jesus'. On the basis of this claim, Muggleton presents an interpretation of the book of Revelation which is wholly rooted in his rejection of all forms of organized religion. All forms of worship and all ministers are false, he argues, 'from the first Pope to the last Quaker'.

Claiming to be a reluctant prophet, Muggleton argues that people are ignorant because their teachers are ignorant: they 'blind themselves in the knowledge of the true God, and the right devil, and of the true interpretation of the scriptures'. Unlike many interpreters of Revelation, Muggleton sees it as a unified whole. The seven churches of Asia addressed in Revelation 2 and 3 are taken to have their counterparts in seven churches of Europe, who are summoned by seven 'anti-angels'; they begin with the Church of Rome and end with the Quakers, whose ministry, says Muggleton, will last until the end of the world. Given the turmoil of the time, this cannot be far away: 'for is not almost all the world in an uproar, killing and destroying one another, ever since the seventh anti-angel did begin to sound?'

Muggletonianism was very much a product of its time. Since the 1570s the Puritans had been using alternative forms of worship in addition to those prescribed by law in the Prayer Book. Informal prayer meetings abounded, which resulted in a tendency to undermine the exclusivity of formal church worship. After the execution of Charles I in 1648 the Church in England was in disarray, with no generally accepted doctrine. Moreover, as Christopher Hill has pointed out, in the millennial atmosphere of the 1640s it was not hard to accept that God would first reveal things of the end to an Englishman. Muggleton claimed that his interpretation of scripture was infallible, which meant that his designation of himself as a last witness could not be challenged. Despite the death of this 'witness' in 1698 (at the age of 89) his sect lived on. And even today, some extreme brands of evangelicalism are marked by a similar anti-clericalism and anti-intellectualism and a comparable intolerance of any form of biblical interpretation other than their own.

The Last World Emperor

Born in the middle of the fourth century, St Jerome was one of the greatest biblical scholars of his day. He had a hand in virtually the whole of the Latin Bible (later known as the Vulgate), either revising the Latin translation of the Greek New Testament or translating the Old Testament from Hebrew. I have often wished I knew more about him, not least because of his friend, St Paula.

In the later part of their lives Jerome and Paula settled in Bethlehem, where they ran separate establishments for men and women seeking the religious life. It was in Bethlehem, in 407, that St Jerome wrote his commentary on the Old Testament book of Daniel. It is notable for the way in which Jerome recovers neglected Jewish traditions to help his readers understand the meaning of the original author. So, for example, whereas Christian commentators had seen the latter part of Daniel 11 as referring to the persecution of the Jews by Antiochus Epiphanes, Hebrew authorities, according to Jerome, understood it to refer to the Romans. In particular, Daniel 11:33 is interpreted as an allusion to the destruction of the Temple under Vespasian and Titus: 'And those among the people who are wise shall make many understand, though they shall fall by sword and flame, by captivity and plunder, for some days.'

This ties in well with Daniel 7, where Belshazzar's vision of four beasts is interpreted as representing four kingdoms. The fourth beast has ten horns and a further little horn, and Jewish and Christian commentators alike have seen the fourth beast as Rome and the little horn as a future tyrant or Antichrist emerging from it. So the Roman empire was widely believed to be the last great kingdom to exercise worldly power before the end, and we have already seen how the writer of 2 Thessalonians may have regarded Rome as in some way helping to delay the end. What then happens to this belief once Rome had finally fallen in 476? One answer lies in the figure known as the Last World Emperor.

This emperor is a kind of human saviour, whose rule takes place between the period of great tribulation and the coming of Antichrist before the end. His reign resembles a millennial reign of peace, though there is no hint of his being a Christ-like figure and there is no biblical source for him. He seems to appear on the scene first in the fourth century when his activities are recorded in a text known as the Tiburtine Oracle.

When the original Syrian text was composed, the Last World Emperor could still be seen as an emperor of Rome; so the prophet (or sibyl) could move straight from the signs and troubles of the end to the Last World Emperor and all the other eschatological events. The surviving text, however, is an eleventh-century version, which demands the addition of a long list of European kings who are predicted to reign after the fall of Rome, including Lombards and Franks. Finally the Last World Emperor arrives: he stands out from the rest because of his physical appearance and his exploits as a Christian crusader. We then revert to the original text in which this emperor, called Constance, is Greek, and it is prophesied that he will rule over Greeks and Romans for 112 years. He is to convert Egypt and Ethiopia to Christianity and the Jews also are converted. 'In those days,' concludes the oracle, 'Judah will be saved and Israel will live without fear.' In later medieval drama the Last World Emperor is portrayed as controlling the whole world. He then abdicates power, either in the Jerusalem Temple or on the Mount of Olives, leaving the way clear for Antichrist to enter Jerusalem.

Belief in the Last World Emperor persisted throughout the Middle Ages. It ties in with the idea in Revelation that there will be a kingdom of peace on earth before the end. And it also fits in with the views of those who see this period as a metaphor for the age of the church, during which the gospel is preached throughout the world.

An alternative figure to the Last World Emperor is that of the Angelic Pope. He has a similar role, but it is performed by a religious leader rather than a worldly one. Unlike the Last World Emperor, though, he seems to be a purely medieval creation, a consequence, perhaps, of a greater focus on the church and its institutions. In 1184 Joachim di Fiore's *De Prophetia Ignota* predicted that a companion of Elijah would commission a future pope to preach the gospel at the time of persecution immediately before Antichrist's arrival. The American scholar Bernard McGinn has described this as 'perhaps the most significant medieval addition to the apocalyptic scenario'. McGinn also notes the tradition of 'spiritual men' – preachers and contemplatives – who would work alongside the Angelic Pope. This may be one reason why the idea of an Angelic Pope went on to be popular among fifteenth- and sixteenth-century Franciscans, who placed in this figure their hope that the papacy would be reformed, enabling the church to enter a new age.

The returning hero

In the course of the medieval period the figure of the Last World Emperor is frequently developed into a character who is not a new leader, but a heroic one from the past. A great national leader is believed to be about to return before the end, in order to rescue his people in their hour of need, and to usher in the millennial age of peace. As with the Last World Emperor, this does not imply that Christian hopes and ideals are set aside. Typically the heroes combine Christian and secular leadership as anointed kings or emperors. In the Christian West the Holy Roman Emperor was often attributed biblical-type characteristics. The Emperor Charlemagne was described in popular epic poetry as having lived to a great old age and as being in touch with God through visions or angelic visitations. In the case of one hero his very existence is in doubt. I set off in search of him – the legendary King Arthur.

On an exceptionally bleak winter afternoon, with snow clouds heavy on the horizon, the open countryside north of Wimborne Minster in Dorset was not a comfortable place to be. I had left the A35 trunk road, which connects Southampton with the West country, to take a look at Badbury Rings. This is the site of an iron age hill fort, which was probably in use for some 700 years from the sixth century BC. Before that, possibly as long ago as the second or third millennium BC, the site was used for burials. Today the wide concentric rings of ditches and ramparts around a central hillock are still easy to make out. Sheep graze in the grassy ditches and people from Wimborne walk their dogs there. Yet the bitterly cold wind that afternoon was a useful reminder of the original remoteness of the place. It would have been a good place for a battle, and back in the Dark Ages it may well have been just that.

Badbury Rings is one of several possible sites of the battle of Mount Badon, around AD518. Those who fell there were Saxons, whose raids had been proving increasingly troublesome since the Roman forces had begun withdrawing from southern England. The victors, according to a Welsh monk called Nennius writing in the eighth century, were a mixed force of Romans and Britons, and their commander was the ancient British hero, Arthur.

Just as it is hard to identify the site of Arthur's crucial victory with any certainty, it is even more difficult to pinpoint the place where Arthur met his death in another historic battle some twenty years later, which Nennius calls Camlan. Not even the date of Arthur's last battle is known for sure. The twelfth-century chronicler Geoffrey of Monmouth puts it at 542, while the French writer Robert Wace (writing around 1155) dates it a century later. But by the time of Geoffrey and Wace, a significant difference had crept in:

> Arthur... our renowned King, was mortally wounded and was carried off to the Isle of Avalon, so that his wounds might be attended to. He handed the crown of Britain over to his cousin Constantine, the son of Cador Duke of Cornwall.

Arthur was defeated, certainly, but was he dead? Wace takes up the story:

> He is yet in Avalon, awaited of the Britons; for as they say and deem he will return from whence he went and live again... Merlin said of Arthur... that his end should be hidden in doubtfulness. The prophet spoke truly. Men have ever doubted, and – as I am persuaded – will always doubt whether he liveth or is dead.

By the end of the twelfth century Layamon is reporting Arthur's words to Constantine as he gives him the crown:

> I will far to Avalun, to... an elf most fair, and she shall make my wounds all sound... And afterwards I will come again to my kingdom, and dwell with the Britains with mickle [much] joy.

Layamon ends his story by referring the reader back to Merlin: 'He said... that an Arthur should yet come to help the English.'

The Middle Ages is rich in tales of King Arthur and his Knights of the Round Table. The stories are most highly developed in French literature, and it is not surprising to find that, given the general hostility between France and England, these writers play down the idea of a national hero returning to help the English in their hour of need. Even so, the anonymous thirteenth-century writer of *The Death of King Arthur* ('La Mort le Roi Artu') does not describe Arthur's actual death, though a tombstone inscription, 'Here lies King Arthur, who conquered twelve kingdoms', is a fair indication that he thought it took place.

The mainstream English tradition, though, expresses the hope, if not always the certain expectation, that Arthur will return. The historical Arthur is a shadowy, distant figure: the date of his death is uncertain, as is the place of his greatest battle at 'Mount Badon'. It may be that he never existed at all, or at least not as a great king ruling over a near idyllic kingdom, as later legend has him. But from that obscure beginning, Arthur evolves into a figure of such stature that his return from the dead is anticipated at the hour of his people's greatest need. In short, he is thrust into the tradition of a great figure who will appear before the end of time, and is probably the first of a number of national leaders who emerge with this role from different nations at a given point in their history.

Malory's *Morte d'Arthur* (1485) gives Arthur a wider significance than simply a national saviour – he resembles a Christian crusader:

> Yet some men say in many parts of England that King Arthur is not dead, but had by the will of our Lord Jesu into another place; and men say that he shall come again and he shall win the holy cross... Many men say that there is written upon his tomb this verse: HIC IACET ARTHURUS, REX QUONDAM REXQUE FUTURUS. [Here lies Arthur, the once and future king.] (Bk 21, ch. 7).

Later tradition, though, is divided as to how it views Arthur. One strand retains the idea of a national leader but instead of the original Arthur emerging from the mists of Avalon, he is to be embodied in a contemporary leader, typically a British king. James I, Charles II and the Duke of Wellington (Sir Arthur Wellesley) were all acclaimed as Arthur in their time, and the name itself is a popular one in royal circles, even in modern times. Queen Victoria named her seventh child Arthur (he was the Duke of Wellington's godson) and the present Prince of Wales also bears the name.

This treatment of the ancient legend reveals a characteristic feature of unfulfilled (and possibly unfulfillable) prophecy: constant reinterpretation.

Popular tradition held that Arthur would return in the nation's hour of need but he failed to come; therefore it must really mean that he would return in the form of somebody else. All you have to do is choose your leader. If that leader fails to come up to expectations, then wait for the next one.

In a different development of the Arthurian tradition, interest is focused less on Arthur himself and more on his kingdom. According to this view, the age of chivalry is a lost paradise – a world of social order and high ideals, as embodied in the Round Table knights. There are obvious parallels here with millennial thought and the longing for a future paradise on earth. Anyone who knew the legend in sufficient detail may also have seen a similarity between the collapse of Arthur's kingdom because of the evil within (Queen Guinevere's adulterous and ultimately tragic relationship with Lancelot) and the Fall, brought about by the serpent in the Garden of Eden.

The identification of Arthur with a lost social order and the longing for its return was particularly evident in nineteenth-century England, where it inspired a number of literary and artistic works, not all of them of equal merit.

> Arthur, the father of Chivalry's fights
> His heroes and bards, and his round-table knights,
> Not wrong were the legends, or prophecy's strain
> Which told that King Arthur should yet rise again.

This piece of near doggerel, from a collection of poems on Welsh subjects by T.J. Llewelyn Prichard in *The Cambrian Wreath* (1828), is fairly typical of the genre. Tennyson, who is sometimes held responsible for a wave of Arthurian fervour in Victorian times, describes Arthur returning on Christmas morning, thereby symbolizing a Christian birth in a time when faith was thought to be in decline (*The Epic*). In the *Idylls of the King* the same poet looks back to the achievement of the historical Arthur in unifying the kingdom, outlawing the destructive forces of warring princes:

> ...Arthur and his knighthood for a space
> Were all one will, and through that strength the King
> Drew in the petty princedoms under him,
> Fought, and in twelve great battles overcame
> The heathen hordes, and made a realm and reign'd.
> (*Coming of Arthur*)

At the end of this epic, before Arthur leaves for Avalon, Sir Bedivere comments on the end of the Arthurian age: 'Now I see the true old times are dead.'

It was a longing for the return of those 'true old times' that probably led to Arthur and his court becoming a popular subject for artists in the late Victorian age and into the twentieth century. Foremost among these artists were the Pre-Raphaelites William Morris and Edward Burne-Jones (who is said to have kept Malory's *Morte d'Arthur* at his side throughout his life). Burne-Jones was also a Tractarian, and for him the Arthurian legend of the quest for the holy grail was particularly meaningful. For both artists, Arthurian subjects, especially as they were depicted in medieval literature, represented a return to a lost idyllic past. As Harrison and Waters put it: 'Medievalism was… a total way of life… a desire to search out and return beauty to an age from which it seemed to have disappeared. [Morris and Burne-Jones] felt that in the Middle Ages life and art were closer to nature and therefore less corrupt.' For seventeen years, between 1881 and 1898, Burne-Jones worked on a painting called 'The Sleep of King Arthur in Avalon', in which the sleeping (not dead) Arthur is attended by the queens who had brought him there. Now in a museum in Puerto Rico, it is strongly suggestive of the belief that sleep will end in renewal.

Such was the popularity of Arthurian themes at this time that one critic has estimated that a single decade (1860–69) produced fifty to sixty paintings with Arthurian subjects. This is echoed by the number of 'Arthurian' films in the twentieth century – around forty since the first appeared in 1904, which was a film of Wagner's *Parsifal*. The films, though, have little to contribute to the portrayal of Arthur's court as a lost paradise, and still less to the theme of Arthur's return. One of the more recent, and possibly the most sentimental, the musical *Camelot*, does not even go as far as the final battle, with only the closing music hinting at eventual doom.

The Arthurian legends are excellent stories and they owe much of their power to the fact that when they were written down no one doubted that Arthur was a real historical figure. The changing interpretation of these stories at different periods reflects the concerns of those times. And foremost among these has been the desire for a lost hero to return to his people at a turning point in their history and a longing for the return of that earthly paradise that Arthur's world represents.

Some other lost heroes are less elusive than the mysterious Arthur, but their stories are just as romantic, not to say far-fetched. One such hero is the twelfth-century German emperor Frederick Barbarossa. Legend has it that he never died but lies asleep inside the Kyffhäuser mountain, some fifty to sixty miles west of Leipzig. The truth is more mundane: Frederick died in 1190 while on crusade – his body was dragged from a river in Asia Minor and there was no suggestion that he was still alive.

The story surrounding Barbarossa emerged after the death of his grandson, Emperor Frederick II, in 1250. The date is important because of the strong belief at the time that the world would end in 1260. If Frederick II was therefore to be seen as the Emperor of the Last Days, it followed that people should support his successor, Conrad IV, in the expectation that the glorious reign would continue. The rumour that Frederick Barbarossa was not really dead seems to have been started for purely political reasons by the people of Tivoli, who were afraid of Conrad. As the rumour grew and the legend developed, the two Fredericks became hopelessly confused in popular tradition. For centuries stories circulated about the return of the 'good emperor' Frederick – rather like Arthur – at a time of national crisis. Kyffhäuser even became a place of Christian pilgrimage before the Reformation, with pilgrims hoping they would be able to exorcize the emperor's ghost.

The myth that had a political origin continued to be used for political ends in the nineteenth century, when Frederick was expected to return and defeat Napoleon, a victory which might then result in the restoration of the empire or a united Germany. This is not so far removed from the Victorians' hope of a new Arthurian age. In each case secular ambitions sought support and justification from a familiar religious model of the return of a superhuman character to inaugurate a time of peace and prosperity – a new Eden.

A final example of a returning hero is someone who lived 400 years after Frederick Barbarossa. He was Dom Sebastião (Sebastian), who became King of Portugal in 1554 at the age of three. Sebastian's death when he was still in his twenties was almost entirely of his own making, but like Arthur no one seems to have actually seen him die. Sebastian's ambition was to drive the forces of Islam out of Africa and establish Christianity there. After an initial victory at Tangiers, Sebastian assembled an army of mercenaries at Alcacer-el-Kabir. Leading from the front the king charged into battle, but forgot to give the order to his battalions to follow. The Portuguese were massacred but the king fought off attempts both by his own side and by the opposition to rescue him from the confusion – hence the absence of Portuguese witnesses to his death, though his body was eventually retrieved from the battlefield. Many believed that Sebastian had escaped and he too became the subject of a 'lost hero' legend, with crusading overtones, which survived until the nineteenth century.

Antichrist

Prophets and ancient heroes returning from the dead are the nice guys of the end-time. The very last person to appear on the world stage is the embodiment of evil: Antichrist. Popularly portrayed as the son of a human mother and satanic father, Antichrist is the evil counterpart to Jesus Christ. While the human Jesus is total goodness, Antichrist is wholly evil; according to the so-called 'doctrine of recapitulation' formulated by Irenaeus in the late second century, all the past evils of history are to be concentrated in him.

Unlike the Last World Emperor, there are some possible precedents in both the Hebrew and Christian scriptures for the person of Antichrist, although scholars disagree on the details. Both Jewish and Christian traditions have the idea of a tyrant who is to appear at the end. In apocalyptic writing, he can be seen in Daniel 7, where the final king of the fourth kingdom (the 'little horn') is set apart from the rest:

> He shall speak words against the Most High,
> and shall wear out the saints of the Most High,
> and shall think to change the times and the law;
> and they shall be given into his hand
> for a time, two times, and half a time.

In Revelation 13 the beast from the sea has a similar function, with some added details: the beast is worshipped (v. 4) because it is invincible, and worshippers have its number – 666 – marked on them (vv. 16-17); it pronounces blasphemies against God (v. 6); it wages war on the saints and conquers them (v. 7) and eventually has the whole earth in its power (vv. 7-8).

In non-apocalyptic Christian writing, Antichrist is simply an opponent or usurper of the faith. So the writer of 1 John refers to 'many antichrists' (1 John 2:18) who seem to be people who have broken away from the Christian community. They are defined by opposition: 'This is antichrist, he who denies the Father and the Son' (v. 22). The context suggests that these opponents did not deny God the Father, and this may explain a strand of the tradition where Antichrist is Jewish. The 'man of lawlessness' of 2 Thessalonians 2:3 who must come before the end goes further in his blasphemy. He 'opposes and exalts himself against every so-called god or object of worship, so that he takes his seat in the temple of God, proclaiming himself to be God' (2:4). The writer also describes how he will have miraculous powers (given him by Satan) and will be able to deceive some of the faithful (2:9-10).

These references are not enough on their own to provide the powerful and elaborate tradition of Antichrist which emerges in the early centuries of Christianity. But rather like a giant snowball these literal and figurative expressions of opposition gather up with them other visions of evil from both the past and the present. So Antichrist slips easily into the place already occupied by Satan in Jewish scripture. In Isaiah 14 the King of Babylon is addressed as if he were Satan himself, revealing how the devil was depicted at the time:

> You said in your heart,
> 'I will ascend to heaven;
> above the stars of God
> I will set my throne on high…
> I will ascend above the heights of the clouds,
> I will make myself like the Most High…'
> Those who see you will stare at you,
> and ponder over you:
> 'Is this the man who made the earth tremble,
> who shook kingdoms,
> who made the world like a desert
> and overthrew its cities…' (Isaiah 14:13,14, 16-17).

These features of an evil king/Satan setting himself over and above God and overpowering earthly kingdoms are readily transferred to Antichrist.

Other evil figures who flit in and out of Hebrew and Christian scriptures and non-canonical writing also have a contribution to make to the picture of wickedness. In particular there is Belial (or Beliar), originally a Jewish figure who is so evil that when he occurs in Psalm 18, modern translators couple him with death and give him the name 'perdition':

> The cords of death encompassed me
> the torrents of perdition assailed me (Psalm 18:4).

One suggestion is that 'Belial' is derived from the Hebrew verb 'to engulf', and so had the original meaning of someone who engulfs others, that is, in hell.

The fourth-century apocryphal book *The Ascension of Isaiah* is one of those texts which probably start off Jewish (with an account of the legend of Isaiah's martyrdom) and end up Christian (with a section describing a vision of Isaiah which includes the death and resurrection of Christ and the events of the end). In this later section Beliar appears as Satan who comes to earth at the end as Antichrist:

> At the consummation Beliar, the great prince, will come down, the king of this world, who has had dominion over it since it first came into being: he will come down from his abode in the vault of heaven in the form of a man, as a lawless king and a matricide. And this king will persecute the plant which the twelve apostles of the Beloved have planted... At his command the sun will rise during the night, and he will make the moon appear at midday. And he will have his own way in the world over everything: he will act and speak like the Beloved and will say, It is I who am the Lord... (IV:2-3, 5-6).

In Beliar, then, we have a satanic figure from Jewish mythology ready to be combined with early Christian ideas on the end, particularly the belief that Antichrist will pass himself off as Christ and deceive the Christian faithful.

A final strand in the biblical pattern of wickedness comes a couple of centuries later, when Gregory the Great in his *Moralia* identifies the Old Testament monsters Leviathan and Behemoth as symbols of Antichrist and the devil respectively. This added detail suggests, in line with Revelation, that Satan or Antichrist is temporarily out of the way or 'bound', only to reappear when the end-time comes. As Isaiah promised:

> In that day the Lord with his hard and great and strong sword will punish Leviathan the fleeing serpent, Leviathan the twisting serpent, and he will slay the dragon that is in the sea (Isaiah 27:1).

Added to this tradition are examples of evil personified in real life. Two people who readily find a place in the build-up of Antichrist are the Greek tyrant Antiochus IV Epiphanes who persecuted the Jews, and the Roman Emperor Nero who did the same to the Christians. The popular legend that Nero was not dead and would return as a great tyrant at a future date no doubt also helped to build up a vivid picture in people's minds of the unparalleled evil of the figure who would bring about the world's destruction. Augustine tried to counter this belief: 'I wonder that men can be so audacious in their conjectures,' he wrote damningly.

Even in New Testament times it seems as though writers were using the term 'antichrist' without further explanation, which suggests that people were already familiar with its meaning. Certainly the tradition seems to have been established very quickly with little variation. The fourth-century Tiburtine oracle describes how Antichrist, the Prince of Iniquity, will be revealed as soon as the Last World Emperor has surrendered his crown at Jerusalem. He then murders Elijah and Enoch (though they are resurrected after three days) and follows this with unprecedented persecution. The end comes when the Archangel Michael kills Antichrist on the Mount of Olives.

In the tenth century Adson de Montier-en-Der wrote a *Treatise on Antichrist*, giving him a whole life story, from his conception by the devil and his birth in Babylon (the city epitomizing evil), through to the last days. The dramatic potential of all this was largely confined to the mystery plays of the later Middle Ages, but the identification of hated people and institutions with Antichrist has persisted down the centuries to our own times.

Inevitably there is disappointment in store when 'Antichrist' continues to prosper despite claims that a rival institution will cause his downfall. Great claims were made for the Reformation on this score, in the hope that it would lead to the downfall of the pope in Rome. Even as late as 1784 one William Richards wrote: 'The Reformation... was an event that gave a terrible blow to the kingdom of Antichrist. Like the confusion at Babel, it broke a most cursed confederacy.' But by then the idea that the Antichrist pope would be overthrown by Protestants had been reworked and other contenders for the role of Antichrist had emerged. Richards appeals to the concept of several antichrists from 1 John, and on this basis elaborates a theory of 'antichristianity'. This enables him to add his own hobby-horses to his hatred of the papacy and of Roman Catholic doctrines. Well to the fore are churches which practise infant baptism: he doubts whether

there be... in the whole pestilential group of antichristian institutions, by which the son of perdition maintains his influence in the world, any one thing so subservient to the interest of that hateful potentate, so extensive in its mischief, or, even so repugnant, in every point of view to the design and spirit of the New Testament, as infant sprinkling.

Subsequently he defined the antichristian kingdom as a 'kingdom of the clergy' and concluded that the 'Spirit of Antichrist' 'appears to be no other than the spirit of the world in disguise'.

Richards' prose, despite its eighteenth-century style, is very little different from many polemics written 200 years later. And in some respects his bigotry is more logical than, say, the superstitions of those who looked askance at the American President with the three six-letter names Ronald Wilson Reagan, or indeed that President himself, who changed the number of his home from 666 (the mark of the beast in Revelation 13:18, commonly understood to be the translation of a human name into numerical terms) to 668.

Gog and Magog

By now the end-time scenario begins to appear somewhat crowded, but there are still hordes of people of the end to come. These are the forces of Gog and Magog, who first appear in Ezekiel 38. Here Gog is the wicked ruler of the land of Magog who is used by God to launch a terrible attack against Israel. This provokes an apocalyptic catastrophe:

> On that day there shall be a great shaking in the land of Israel; the fish of the sea and the birds of the air, and the beasts of the field, and all creeping things that creep on the ground, and all the men that are upon the face of the earth, shall quake at my presence, and the mountains shall be thrown down, and the cliffs shall fall, and every wall shall tumble to the ground. I will summon every kind of terror against Gog, says the Lord God; every man's sword will be against his brother. With pestilence and bloodshed I will enter into judgment with him; and I will rain upon him and his hordes and the many people that are with him, torrential rains and hailstones, fire and brimstone (Ezekiel 38:19-22).

These armies reappear in Revelation 20 (where Magog is now a separate force) as the agents of Satan in waging the final battle:

> When the thousand years are ended, Satan will be loosed from his prison and will come out to deceive the nations which are at the four

corners of the earth, that is, Gog and Magog, to gather them for battle (Revelation 20:7-8).

An onslaught led by these armies came to be expected before the reign of Antichrist. And just as Antichrist has been identified with hated rulers, so Gog and Magog have been identified with hated powers, from the Goths and the Huns in the Dark Ages to the Russians in the twentieth-century Cold War. More generally, Gog and Magog have been seen not as specific nations but as agents of the persecution of Christians before the end. Augustine, though, proposed an allegorical interpretation: Gog represents people whose hearts are ruled by the devil, while Magog is the devil himself.

As successive ages sought to identify these people of the end from their own or future generations, a further element had to be taken into account. In order to show that the signs and the people of the end were in place, one more question had to be answered: the question of whether the time too was right.

References

M. Ashley, *England in the Seventeenth Century*, Penguin Books, 1952.

Richard Kenneth Emmerson, *Antichrist in the Middle Ages – A Study of Medieval Apocalypticism, Art and Literature*, Seattle, 1981.

J. Bowerman, *Jerome's Commentary on Daniel*, Washington DC, 1978.

Geoffrey of Monmouth, *The History of the Kings of Britain*, translated Lewis Thorpe, Penguin Books, 1966.

Martin Harrison and Bill Waters, *Burne-Jones*, London, 1973, p. 45.

Christopher Hill, 'John Reeve and the Origins of Muggletonianism' in A. Williams (editor), *Prophecy and Millenarianism – Essays in Honour of Marjorie Reeves*, Longman, 1980.

Thomas Mallory, *Le Morte d'Arthur*, 2 volumes, edited by Janet Cowen, Penguin Books, 1969.

J.R.H. Moorman, *A History of the Church in England*, A&C Black, 3rd edition, 1980.

Ludowick Muggleton, *A true interpretation of all the chief texts and mysterious sayings and visions opened of the whole book of the Revelation of St John*, 1665; reprinted London, 1808.

William Richards, *The History of Antichrist, or, Free Thoughts on the Corruptions of Christianity*, Lynn, Norfolk, 1784.

Wace and Layamon, *Arthurian Chronicles*, translated by Eugene Mason, J.M. Dent & Sons, 1962.

Chapter 6

Times of the End

'Jesus said: "Of that day and hour no one knows, not even the angels of heaven, but the Father only."'

Matthew 24:36

'They question you about the Hour of Doom. "When will it come?" they ask. But how are you to know? Only your Lord knows when it will come. Your duty is but to warn those that fear it.'

Koran, 79:46

'I do believe that the Lord will come down when the end of the world is near. But I still believe that it is a long way off yet.'

Joseph Neary, aged 12

The timing of the end is known only to God. On that the Christian gospels and the Islamic scriptures agree. Yet central to human beings' historical obsession with the end of the world is a tireless effort to work out when it will happen. As quickly as one calculation proves false, another comes along to replace it. It is as if the drama of humankind's failure to obey the ancient command not to eat the fruit of the tree of knowledge in the Garden of Eden is being perpetually re-enacted. Perhaps the purveyors of the old creation myths were wiser than we give them credit for.

Broadly speaking, attempts to determine the time of the end fall into two categories. There are, on the one hand, dates which depend on a structure. This may take the form of dividing the whole time span of the created world into periods of a fixed length, with the events of the end coming at or near to the close of the final period. Other structures may depend on a specific event, which in Christianity is the birth – or sometimes the crucifixion – of Jesus. This has often been seen as taking place in the centre of time; once the length of time between creation and Christ is determined, the date of the end can also be known.

The second category of dates is less logical. These are timings which depend on the interpretation of prophecy, usually from apocalyptic writing, which is typically given in imprecise terms. Attempts to decipher the hidden 'meaning' of number symbolism and to relate the resulting calculations to actual events account for some of the more bizarre interpretations of the end. I should say here that I have no particular axe to grind. I believe that the 'numbers' of biblical and intertestamental apocalyptic are metaphors, not to be taken literally, and I have no difficulty with Jesus' statement that God alone knows when the end will come. But I marvel at the ingenuity of some of the arguments put forward – against all the odds – for particular dates. This obsession with the time as much as with the manner of the end is a telling, and sometimes amusing, demonstration of human foolishness in the face of both divine wisdom and scientific evidence.

Playing with numbers

Many if not most predictions as to when the world will end involve a numbers game. Sometimes playing with numbers will produce a date, which then leads people to look for the relevant signs and events to confirm it. At other times, things seem to be the other way about: it would suit someone to predict the end of the world at a certain time, so the numbers are manipulated in order to produce the right moment. More often than not it is impossible to say which came first – the sign or the date: an eschatological chicken and egg situation.

In seventeenth-century Protestant England 1656 was a popular date for the end, thanks to the parallelism with the flood, which had been put at 1656 years after creation. This was undeniably a date that suited both religious and political propagandists. In particular it helped with the Jewish 'problem'. Jews had long since been expelled from England, and in 1648 there was a pogrom in the Ukraine. To admit Ukrainian Jews to England, it was argued, would speed up their conversion and bring about the last days.

The English expansionist policy in America was justified in much the same way. There was a theory that some American Indians were descendants of the lost tribes of Israel. Colonization, therefore, would serve the same end of hastening the end-time. The historian Christopher Hill has pointed out that there was no significant conversion of the Jews by 1656 (though they had been admitted to England by then), but the result was certainly a boost for English foreign policy.

If that reasoning seems to have only a tenuous link with biblical sources, other uses of numbers are even more suspect. There is, for example, the argument of Pareus. By redating the destruction of Jerusalem from AD70 to AD73, he was able to argue not only that this had introduced the millennium, but – more relevantly – that the thousand years would end in 1073, the year Gregory VII was elevated to the see of Rome.

Using numbers like this can be traced back to very ancient origins. When the 'Preacher' of Ecclesiastes wrote, 'What has been done is what will be done, and there is nothing new under the sun,' he was probably not as world-weary as he sounds. Rather, his statement may well reflect the influence of Babylonian astrology. The Babylonians did not see history as having a beginning and an end. For them, the pattern of history was a never-ending cycle; but unlike, say, today's Hindus, the Babylonians did not envisage the wheel of life constantly turning in a cycle of birth, death and rebirth or reincarnation. Their wheel went round and then turned back again. Each time the wheel changed direction this was marked by catastrophic events. On the first turn everything proceeded normally, but on the wheel's return everything ran backwards: human beings were born old and grew younger, moving towards a golden age. The two ages were said to last 36,000 years and the cycle is to be repeated as long as the universe exists.

Such a view of history could not be sustained alongside the Jewish belief in God as the creator of all life, particularly since in the Babylonian system humans in the golden age were born of the earth and sustained by it. But we have already seen that the influence of the Babylonians is felt through Jewish apocalyptic writing and beyond it. In particular they handed on their fascination with numbers and the measurement of time based on the movement of the sun and moon, as well as the way in which they envisaged apocalyptic chaos. But since their revolving world was never-ending, for them there truly was nothing new under the sun.

A further possible legacy of the Babylonians is the special importance they attributed to the number four. This was taken up by the Greeks and is reflected, among other things, in their identification of the four elements that make life on earth possible. The four kingdoms represented by four beasts in Daniel 7 may therefore be taken to indicate completeness: after them only the end remains.

The model of creation

In Jewish tradition the seven-day week is fundamental to measuring time. The Genesis account of God creating the world in six days and resting on the seventh is a model not just for the working week and the sabbath, but for calculating the structure of time itself.

At one level the week is a unit of measurement: a week of years is seven years; when multiplied by seven this produces another time unit of forty-nine years, to which is added a fiftieth 'jubilee' year. According to Leviticus 25, this jubilee year is a holy year in which there is to be no heavy farming activity, rather like the sabbath rest in an ordinary week. But before long the word jubilee came to mean not the fiftieth year, but the forty-nine-year period of time that preceded it. This is commonly rounded up to include the fiftieth year, which usefully fits in with measurements in decades. Calculations based on this unit of the jubilee provide the structure for the first-century BC book of Jubilees, which attempts to put a date on many of the events familiar to us from Genesis.

The jubilees provide a dating for the time of creation, which is done by working backwards from the Israelites' entry into the promised land of Canaan, dated as fifty jubilees from creation (or 2,450 years) – the jubilee of jubilees. The compiler of Jubilees does not, though, spell out a date for the end of time as well:

The Jubilees shall pass by till Israel is cleansed from all guilt of fornication, and uncleanness, and pollution, and sin, and error, and dwells in safety in all the land; and there shall no longer be an adversary or any evil power to afflict them and the land shall be clean from that day forward for evermore (Jubilees 50:5).

An alternative dating uses the Jews' exodus from Egypt as the pivotal event, forty years before Israel reached the promised land. Some scholars have suggested that, following the lists of generations in Genesis 11, the Exodus can be dated at 2,666 years from creation. If this is combined with the view said to emerge from one of the four sources of Genesis (the so-called Priestly source which dates from around 500BC), that the world will last 4,000 years from creation, then the Exodus comes two-thirds of the way through. Under this scheme, the world could be expected to end around the time that, as it happens, saw the persecution of the Jews by Antiochus, the revolt of the Maccabees, and the writing of the Book of Daniel: all in the 160s BC.

The Essenes

At the time of the birth of Christ, when expectations of a Jewish Messiah were running high, different groups made their own calculations as to when the Messiah would come. The Pharisees, Zealots and Essenes all based their calculations on Daniel's prophecy of seventy weeks of years. But because each group started from slightly different versions of the text, they all came up with different dates. And after the destruction of the Temple in AD70, some Jewish interpreters ceased to see the prophecy as relating to the Messiah at all.

Of these groups, the most significant is the Essenes, whom we have already encountered as the only key Jewish apocalyptic sect of the first century, besides the early Christians. From the scrolls discovered in the Qumran caves we know that the book of Jubilees and the Ethiopic book of 1 Enoch were particularly important texts for this sect, as well as their own writings. Research published by Dr Roger Beckwith has uncovered the Essenes' fascination with numbers and their calculations of significant end-time events.

One of the documents found in fragments at Qumran portrays Melchizedek (seen as the same figure as the Archangel Michael) as presiding over the last judgment. This is expected to take place on the Day of Atonement at the end of the tenth jubilee of the period of wickedness. Without the rounding up, a period of ten jubilees is 490 years – the equivalent of Daniel's seventy weeks of years, which suggests that this was a standard period at the time. Beckwith points out that the Messiah was expected in the seventh week of the tenth jubilee, which roughly corresponds to the year of Christ's birth (between 3BC and AD2).

According to Roger Beckwith, the Essenes expected the world to end 4,900 years after creation (that is, a jubilee of jubilees twice over). This makes the entry into the promised land (after the first 2,450-year period) the central point in their chronology, comparable to those Christian schemes which have the birth of Jesus at their centre. In modern terms, this suggests that the Essenes expected the end to come in the latter part of the tenth century AD (974–78), which is rather earlier than the Pharisees, who expected the end to come 6,000 years after creation (which they dated 150 later). These Jewish calculations reveal a preoccupation with numbers which is really not justified in terms of sources such as the book of Daniel, and highlights what Beckwith calls a contrast between 'the imprecision of Daniel 9 and the over-precision of all its ancient interpreters'. This, though, goes on to be a characteristic feature of Christian reckoning as well.

The picture changes when the six days of creation are used as a model for the whole span of time. Here the creation story is taken in conjunction with a verse from Psalm 90:

> A thousand years in thy sight
> are but as yesterday when it is past… (Psalm 90:4).

In other words, a 'day' of creation can be taken to represent 1,000 years. From this it is a short step to believing that the world itself will last for 6,000 years, while the final millennium represents God's reign of peace at the end of time. This doctrine (which comes to be known as 'sabbatical millenarianism') is taken over by the early church, with Irenaeus declaring, around AD185, that 'the seventh day is the seventh millennium, the kingdom of the just'. The idea that the world would last for 7,000 years may also have some connection with the astrologers of Ancient Babylon, with their observations of the seven known planets.

Christian arithmetic

In the seventeenth century, the Archbishop of Armagh, James Ussher, calculated that creation took place in the year 4004BC (on 23 October, to be precise) – and until quite recently that date appeared in the margin of the Authorised Version of the Bible. In accordance with tradition Ussher declared that the world would end 6,000 years later, on 23 October 1996, at

6.00 p.m. When that day passed, Richard Dawkins, Oxford's Professor of the Public Understanding of Science and professional atheist, commented: 'What staggers me about Archbishop Ussher's statement is not that he was wrong – so was everybody else in his time – but that he was wrong with such confident and ludicrous precision.' Those of a more cautious disposition pointed out that Ussher had based his calculations on the Julian calendar, which is thirteen days ahead of our Gregorian calendar. But the world did not end on 4 November 1996 either.

Fifteen centuries before Ussher, the early church had set creation slightly earlier. By the fourth century two rival calculations were doing the rounds. Hippolytus of Rome had already put Christ's birth at 5,500 years after creation, which meant that the end was then only a couple of hundred years away. Then, around AD303, Eusebius came up with a more precise date: Christ's ministry (not his birth) began 5,228 years after creation, which gave the church another 500 years before the end.

In spite of strenuous efforts by the church to quash millennial speculation, the idea that Jesus was born 5,500 years after Adam is a popular one in fourth- and fifth-century writing. And when Clement of Alexandria suggested that this period should be 5,600 years instead, a number of possible dates for the end were proposed between the years AD350 and 400.

Two things put an end to these calculations, which were based largely on the estimated timing of Old Testament events. The first was the influence of leading churchmen. Augustine stated in his *City of God* that although he once believed that the world would end after 6,000 years and be followed by a 1,000-year sabbatical rest, he was now arguing that the number 1,000 was purely symbolic – 'an equivalent for the whole duration of the world, employing the number of perfection to mark the fullness of time. For a thousand is the cube of ten.' Augustine's stand against apocalyptic fantasies was so effective, that there is no written evidence of any excitement surrounding the year AD500 when it came, although this does not necessarily mean that the idea of it being the last year had dropped out of popular thinking.

Then St Jerome in his *Commentary on Daniel* argued against the idea of an earthly millennium on the seventh 'day'. He observed sternly, 'The Saints will in no wise have an earthly kingdom, but only a celestial one; this must cease the fable of one thousand years' – and indeed that 'fable' disappeared until well into the Middle Ages.

Yet against all the odds, the ancient dating of the world has survived into modern times, particularly among Christians who cling to the belief that the Bible is 'literally true'. For them the year 2000 has a particular significance. Because if – contrary to overwhelming scientific evidence – creation is put at 4000BC, and if God has a 7,000-year plan for humankind, then the final millennium is imminent. An equally dubious argument (put about by one James McKeever) is that history is divided into 2,000-year periods. The first two periods are from Adam to Abraham and from Abraham to Jesus, while the third is from the first to the Second Coming of Christ. Once again the year 2000 is made to assume – for no very good reason – a quite disproportionate significance.

The other factor was, in a way, much simpler and much more important. It is easy to forget that until the sixth century AD, the usual way of counting years was with reference to a hypothetical starting date for the whole world. All this changed with the introduction of a much more reliable system, which counted from the supposed date of Christ's birth (and where the margin of error was only a few years). Suddenly the old dates lost their significance, and were replaced with new ones. By the time Charlemagne was crowned Holy Roman Emperor on Christmas Day 800, no one apparently made the link with what, under Eusebius' scheme, would have been the beginning of the seventh millennium, though in the latter part of the eighth century a number of 'signs of the end' had been recorded. From now on, Christian calculations of the time of the end were to owe more to New Testament thought than to the Old.

Time with a structure

A structured view of history – as having a beginning, a middle and an end – is at least as old as Zoroastrianism, and some thinkers have tried to divide history into three parts accordingly. An alternative structure emerges from the idea of successive ages, in the course of which human life either moves towards a climax of achievement or degenerates into evil, depending on the thinker's point of view.

Structures of historical periods or 'ages' tend to depend on ingenuity – in the definition of these periods and their dates – just as much as prophecies which fix a precise year for the end. The thought behind them, though, is usually more complex and wide-ranging than is the case with predictions geared solely to a particular date. One system that appears to have been particularly influential is that evolved by Joachim di Fiore in the twelfth century, who divided history into three ages, the third of which was yet to come. Thanks largely to the work done by Marjorie Reeves in researching Joachim's writings, scholars have come to appreciate the extent of his influence during the centuries that followed.

Joachim was born in Calabria in 1135 and became a Cistercian monk. The time is important. On the one hand, speculation that the world would end 1,000 years after Christ's birth, or possibly after the crucifixion, is well in the past. (Indeed, that speculation may not have amounted to very much at all: current thinking is that the significance of the year AD1000 has been exaggerated by earlier historians.) On the other hand, though, a further significant date lay ahead in the not too distant future: the year 1260.

Belief that this particular year would mark the end stems from Revelation 12. There John's vision is of a child who was 'caught up to God and to his throne' (v. 5). The woman who bore him flees to the wilderness, 'where she has a place prepared by God, in which to be nourished for 1,260 days' (v. 6). If the baby is Christ and the mystical female figure is Mary, then the 1,260 days (if days symbolize years) can be interpreted as the age of the church before the end. Joachim reinforced this argument by noting that 1,260 is a multiple of forty-two and thirty. So, since there are forty-two generations between Abraham and Christ (Matthew 1) and if a generation is thirty years, we have another case of symmetry. There are 1,260 years from Abraham to Christ and the same period from Christ's first coming to his return.

Behind these details is a more general scheme of things. Joachim was addressing a common question in the Middle Ages, which is whether there is progress in history, or whether we are simply in a waiting period between Christ's first and second coming. In examining the scriptures, Joachim was looking for clues to the whole meaning of history and focused particularly on symbols, including number symbolism. His writings are very far from being an easy read. He presents time as being divided into three: periods of the Father, Son and Holy Spirit. The first two periods last for sixty-three generations; the third has not yet begun. But, confusingly, there are other divisions within this scheme. Joachim took up Augustine's division of history into seven ages from creation to the end. But history can also be divided into periods of war, in which Satan persecutes the people of God, followed by times of peace. One example he gives is the period of war that stretches from Moses to David, followed by peace during which Solomon builds the Temple. The history of Israel is presented as an example to Christians as to what will happen in the sixth and seventh ages (the seventh and final age begins with the Last World Emperor). Joachim's writing is full of patterns like this, and since his vision of history centres on the church, he sees the church's members and institutions as working for good in the conflict that is to come. The vision of the New Jerusalem in Revelation 20 is for Joachim the seventh age of the church and the third period (*status*) of grace. Bound up with the advent of the final age is the hope of spiritual renewal.

Joachim's main influence may well have been in encouraging a return to symbolic thought systems, though he is especially remembered for his emphasis on Antichrist. Again the timing is significant. Since Augustine, applying Revelation 20 to events of the future had been frowned upon. But the thirteenth century saw a rise in popularity of the book of Revelation and there are many beautifully illuminated copies of it which date from that period. The time was ripe for a return to the ancient symbols, and not least to use them in the hope of determining the exact date of the end.

A new mystical number: three and a half

The prophecy in Daniel 7, which was later taken to refer to the coming of Antichrist, was that the final king of the fourth kingdom would persecute the saints of the Most High 'for a time, two times, and half a time' (Daniel 7:25) – a period most commonly understood to be three and a half years. It has been literally applied to the period when Antiochus' persecution of the Jews was at its most intense, between 167 and 164BC. But in Daniel 12:7, the same expression is used to indicate specifically the length of time before the end. Daniel is told that the troubles will be followed by the resurrection of the dead and he asks, 'How long shall it be till the end of these wonders?' – a question which has been variously taken to refer to the troubles themselves or to the time of resurrection. And the reply comes back, 'for a time, two times, and half a time'.

The special significance of three and a half is of course that it is half the mystical number seven and could be used in much the same way to indicate an indefinite period. The same number crops up again in Revelation in relation to various events of the end which all occur within the same period of three and a half years: the 'nations' 'trample over the holy city for forty-two months' (Revelation 11:2), the Two Witnesses prophesy for 1,260 days (11:3), the woman 'clothed with the sun' flees to the wilderness for 1,260 days (12:6) and the beast exercises authority for forty-two months (13:5). The witnesses who are killed by Antichrist lie dead for three and a half days (11:11) until God restores them to life.

As we have already seen, in the early medieval period the number of days was popularly transferred to years and used to give a date of 1,260 as the end. Others took it more literally and used the three-and-a-half-year period to help pinpoint a more exact date for the end. The three-and-a-half-day period when the witnesses are dead is generally taken to mean just that, probably because of the similarity to the three-day period covering the death and resurrection of Jesus. But the repeated use of these numbers – whether three and a half or 1,260 – in both Daniel and Revelation to refer to different events has led to the number being appropriated by various groups for all kinds of reasons.

Sometimes it appears that any number at all will do to predict the end, regardless of its original meaning. This has been the case with the 'mark of the beast' – 666 – in Revelation 13:18, which has nothing to do with time, although people have not hesitated to use it in that way when it suited them. The year 1666 was regarded as significant by some Protestants whose hopes that the English Civil War heralded the end-time had been dashed by the Restoration of the Monarchy in 1660, when changes to the church and State were reversed. The date of 1666, coupled with astrological phenomena (there was a conjunction of planets in Sagittarius in 1662 and 1666), was sufficient to revive their hopes of the end, at least temporarily.

A Reformer's argument

The Protestant Reformation had a considerable impact on attempts to put a date to the end of time. In England it was widely believed that the English Reformation marked the rising of the Two Witnesses of Revelation 13. But by the time of the Restoration of Charles II, there had emerged a number of scholarly Protestants who, because of their emphasis on judging theology in the light of reason, were inclined to pour scorn on people's attempts to calculate the exact time of the end.

In 1684 an anonymous admirer of Dr Henry More, who was one of a group known as the 'Cambridge Platonists', published a substantial book which set out to answer criticisms of More levied by another anonymous author called simply 'S.E., Mennonite'. Now Mennonites held that the rule of Christ would not come while there remained any earthly monarchs, and one of the aims of the 'Answerer' is to ridicule this belief, which could clearly be used to encourage civil disorder. But, more significantly, the Answerer also seeks to promote the argument that the Protestant Reformation had occurred in the last half of the period of three and a half times of Daniel's prophecy.

The anonymous writer argues, in an appendix entitled *Arithmetica Apocalypta*, that three and a half cannot rationally be translated into an exact period of time such as 1,260 days. How is it, he asks, that Daniel's three and a half (or seven 'semitimes', as he prefers to call it) became the very precise number of 1,260 in Revelation? After all, the 'Spirit of Prophesy' had not in the interim advanced sufficiently to be able to come up with a precise time, which had been impossible before. He suggests a number of reasons in support of his reasoning that this exactness was 'never intended, for so precise an indication of the predicted event, as to limit it to a single year'. The only possible measure is of indeterminate 'prophetical days'. Otherwise, if the 'days' were taken literally, he argues, the 1,260 days of the Two Witnesses would have ended in 1652. Because of the writer's insistence that the Two Witnesses had already come, he is unmerciful in his mockery of those who are still waiting for them and trying to work out when they will arrive. His argument may also have acquired a certain urgency because of another prophecy circulating at the time, which was that the Two Witnesses in fact arose in 1559 but their prophecy was to continue for 127 years, ending in 1686.

The writer does not give any indication as to the length of the final 'semitime' in real time. It will all depend on how the Reformed churches behave themselves: 'The onely true computation of the approach of [Antichrist's] farther fall, and of the farther advancement of the Kingdom of Christ is to be taken from the Christian behaviour of the Reformed churches.' What is more, the Reformed Christian will be marked as being 'inviolably loyal to his Prince'; such behaviour leads to a better estimate of end-time than using numbers.

To some extent these comments must reflect a genuine desire for the symbolism inherent in apocalyptic arithmetic to be more widely recognized. But it also shows what can happen when a precise moment in history is interpreted as one of the events of the end. Everything else must fit. And if numbers do not work, then symbols will.

The power of numbers

There have been many prophecies which do not depend on calculations for the date that they give. The mystique of the turn of a century or of a millennium is sufficient to generate prophecies of the end which give no thought to how the calculation of the time is arrived at. Although it seems now that the year 1000 itself did not produce an undue amount of eschatological anguish, it took only one or two ominous events for people to see themselves as living in the last days. The Danish invasion of England in 1014 was one such event. It occasioned a homily from the preacher Wulfstan which began: 'This world is in haste, it is approaching the end.'

The year 2000, or rather 1999, has been regarded as ominous since the sixteenth century. It was in 1555 that Michel de Nostradame, better known as Nostradamus, published his *Prophéties*. The prophecy for the end of the millennium reads:

> In the year 1999 and seven months,
> from the sky will come the great King of Terror.
> He will bring back to life the great King of the Mongols.
> Before and after, war reigns happily.

If this is seen as having something to do with the end-time – which is not necessarily the case – then this interpretation depends on the use of a date which for some inspires an awe of its own.

Interpreters of Nostradamus have been more than ready to see references to contemporary events in his Delphic utterances and have formulated their own calendars for the end of time. John Hogue, in a book published in 1987, claims that the crunch will come on 5 May 2000, when the new moon aligns with the earth, the sun, Jupiter and Saturn, causing a gravitational tug of war with the five planets on the other side of the sun. To this astrological event he adds a bit of old-fashioned biblical prophecy (the sun and moon will turn red, there will be earthquakes) and that a new age of a new religious consciousness will dawn. Moving onto a grander scale the author predicts that the period between 2000 and 4000 will be 'The Age of

Aquarius', followed by the 'Age of Capricorn' (4000-6000). Meanwhile the world will end in 3797 when the sun will turn into a red giant and earth will be flooded as a result of a collision with a meteor. In the final age (6000-8000), humankind will survive in space.

The division of time into ages, along with the mystique of individual numbers, and a fair dose of far-fetched speculation all have their part to play in predictions of this type. People who indulge in them always have a let-out when things go wrong: it is not they who are mistaken, but the system of interpretation they have applied to the nonsensical pronouncements of a sixteenth-century magician.

An early example of fairly random numbers being used to reinforce beliefs about the end is in the fourth-century work, *The Sibylline Oracles*. This includes the story of how the sibyl interpreted a dream experienced simultaneously by 100 Roman senators. There were nine suns; the first two were bright, the third was the colour of blood and the remainder were increasingly dark, until the ninth sun had only a single ray of light. The idea behind it is that the world is in decay; and it is coupled with a certain temporal structure as well, in that the created world is divided into nine 'generations'. The birth of Christ falls in the fourth age, and the time of the apostolic church in the fifth, both of which temporarily interrupt the process of deterioration.

Beyond arithmetic

Over and against all the attempts to put a more or less exact date to the end of time, it is worth remembering that there are other ways of viewing time. Christian mystics, for example, bear witness to an impulse to rise above time. The Hebrew writers of the Old Testament may well have had a different attitude towards time from our own: they often seem to regard time as determined by the events it contains rather than by an exact measurement.

Similarly, there is more than one way of looking at numbers. For most of us, numbers are the means of imposing order on the world around us: we count and record concrete objects, real events and passing time. But for those with an apocalyptic turn of mind numbers can do something else: they are a means of imposing order on a wholly different kind of reality and thus become symbols of it. As McGinn puts it, 'Numbers not only described, they in some sense revealed the really real.'

In talking about the end, numbers can really only ever make sense as symbols that reveal metaphysical truths. If they are interpreted literally, they are bound to disappoint. Yet, paradoxically, this has never put people off using them. Sociological research has shown that when predicted events fail to materialize, believers will set about with renewed vigour explaining *why* the end did not come, and revising their estimates accordingly. Public, even spectacular, failure has rarely led to a retraction. And the reason for that lies not so much in the arithmetic as in the prophets.

References

An Answer to Several Remarks upon Dr Henry More and his Expositions of the Apocalypse and Daniel, and also upon his apology. Written by S.E., Mennonite. Published in English by The Answerer, 1684.

Roger Beckwith, 'The Significance of the Calendar for Interpreting Essene Chronology and Eschatology', *Revue de Qumran*, May 1980.

Roger Beckwith, 'The Earliest Enoch Literature and its Calendar: Marks of their Origin, Date and Motivation', *Revue de Qumran*, February 1981.

Roger Beckwith, 'Daniel 9 and the Date of Messiah's Coming in Essene, Hellenistic, Pharisaic, Zealot and Early Christian Computation', *Revue de Qumran*, December 1981.

Christopher Hill, '"Till the Conversion of the Jews"', in Richard H. Popkin (editor), *Millenarianism and Messianism in English Literature and Thought, 1650–1800*, E.J. Brill, 1988.

John Hogue, *Nostradamus and the Millennium: Predictions of the Future*, Bloomsbury, 1987.

Bernard McGinn, 'Symbolism in the thought of Joachim of Fiore', in A. Williams (editor), *Prophecy and Millenarianism (Essays in Honour of Marjorie Reeves)*, Longman, 1980.

Marjorie Reeves, *Joachim of Fiore and the Prophetic Future*, SPCK, 1976.

Wulfstan, *The Homilies of Wulfstan*, edited by Bethurum, Clarendon, Oxford, 1957.

Chapter 7

Prophets of the End

'The record of successful prophecy of world events is on a par with the battle honours of the Swiss navy.'

Kevin McClure, *The Fortean Times*, 40

There are many different forms of prophecy and it is true that most prophecies are notable for their failure. This is particularly true of prophecies that are very precise as to when and where certain events will happen. Others are less easy to fault because they are put in more general terms. And still others – like those of Nostradamus – place the whole burden of proof on the interpreter who has to break the prophet's code, and may well get it 'wrong' in the process.

Prophecy is not the same as prediction, although this will often play a part. Down the ages one of the main functions of prophets has been to proclaim the word of God to his people, to warn them about their behaviour, usually making themselves fairly unpopular in the process. This is as true of some leading environmental campaigners today, urging consumers to change their ways, as it was of the Old Testament prophets who exhorted their people to repent and turn back to the Lord. In each case there is the threat of doom if the prophet's words go unheeded.

Central to all this are the prophets themselves. Interestingly, this has always been a role which women have filled as well as men, even in the patriarchal society of Ancient Israel (the Old Testament book of Judges tells the story of Deborah – a prophetess and formidable military campaigner (Judges 4 and 5)). Such women and men have stood out among their contemporaries, prepared to be a lone voice, in order to convey the message which, in the case of religious prophets, they believe to be divinely inspired. Secular prophets have been no less enthusiastic, often risking ridicule and danger for their cause.

Prophets whose message has been mainly concerned with the end of the world are a special breed. The most 'successful' of them have been those who have emerged at times when large sections of society have been anticipating doom or disaster, or at times of heightened eschatological awareness. These prophets (of whom John the Baptist is a prime example) have enjoyed sizeable followings and a considerable personal reputation, and their activities have frequently led to the creation of their own social movements or religious sects. At other times, though, when eschatological expectations have been low, the prophet of the end is isolated and viewed by most as rather weird, an object of curiosity rather than a focus for belief. Yet these brave prophetic souls keep on coming, and they follow in a path that many have trodden before them.

Biblical prophets

The figure of John the Baptist fits many people's idea of what a prophet is like: solitary and rather odd. Mark's gospel opens with a description of John 'in the wilderness' urging people to repent and be baptized:

> John was clothed with camel's hair, and had a leather girdle around his waist, and ate locusts and wild honey (Mark 1:6).

John's message was also – indirectly – a prophecy of the end: 'After me comes he who is mightier than I... I have baptized you with water; but he will baptize you with the Holy Spirit' (Mark 1:7-8). In other words, the Messiah, who was expected to bring the present age to an end, was not far away. Not surprisingly, the Jewish leaders sent people out to discover who he was, this voice 'crying in the wilderness', and their question reveals their perplexity: 'Why are you baptizing, if you are neither the Christ, nor Elijah, nor the prophet?' (John 1:25) ('the prophet', in New Testament terms, being Jesus himself). John's function was to prepare the way for Jesus and he did it through baptism, which had a double significance: it symbolized repentance and was an indication of the believer's readiness to become a follower of the Messiah who was to come.

In his words and actions John is markedly different from the Hebrew prophets who had preceded him centuries before. Some New Testament scholars believe that he was a member of the isolated Qumran community (the sect is known to have practised baptism), which helps to explain his appearance in the wilderness and his unusual clothing. More to the point, this particular community, as we saw in chapter 2, was convinced it was living in the last days before the coming of the Messiah. Moreover, John was the son of Elizabeth (a relation of Mary the mother of Jesus) and of Zechariah who had prophesied at his birth: 'You, child, will be called the prophet of the Most High; for you will go before the Lord to prepare his ways' (Luke 1:76). The son of a prophet, perhaps brought up in a prophetic community, and a blood relative of the human Jesus, John was to be a prophet of the end like no other before or since.

John also stands apart historically from the Hebrew prophets before him. This is because by the first century BC there was a widespread feeling that the voice of prophecy had fallen silent after Malachi, the last of the 'minor' prophets in the Hebrew scriptures. One reason for this may have been the increasingly fixed nature of the canon of scripture; another is certainly the appearance, since the Babylonian exile, of other forms of prophecy or at least of trying to foretell the future. This includes the belief in astrology and cultic oracles beloved of the Babylonians, while the idea that the future is revealed in dreams, albeit to a specially holy person, is commonplace in apocalyptic writing throughout the intertestamental period. Already after the exile (which ended in 538BC) prophecy seemed to be getting a bad name. Through Zechariah, God attacks prophets in Israel, coupling them with idols and unclean spirits:

> I will remove from the land the prophets and the unclean spirit. And if any one again appears as a prophet, his father and mother who bore him will say to him, 'You shall not live, for you speak lies in the name of the Lord' (Zechariah 13:2-3).

In the intertestamental period, though, writers look forward to a new prophet, sometimes identified as the forerunner of the Messiah. The book of 1 Maccabees refers to a future 'trustworthy prophet', while for the Qumran community the Teacher of Righteousness seems to represent a high point in prophecy: in him 'God made known all the mysteries of the words of his servants the prophets' (Commentary on Habakkuk VII).

The apocalyptic writers clearly saw themselves as standing in the line of tradition that stretched from the classical prophets of Ancient Israel to this hope of a final prophet. In a more Spirit-conscious age they shared the same sense of being inspired by God's Spirit and of having a special message to impart. In the New Testament, though, the emphasis is much more on false prophets and their behaviour, perhaps not least because they constituted one of the signs of the end to look out for. And although prophecy is listed by Paul as one of the chief spiritual gifts, it has to be tested to see whether it builds up the Christian fellowship. Those with the gift of prophecy may be perfectly ordinary people; they are to be self-effacing and concerned with encouraging and comforting others (1 Corinthians 14) – not a characteristic generally associated with prophets, whether or not their message has a basis in Christianity. Prophecy, says Paul, should be characterized by being done 'decently and in order' (1 Corinthians 14:40).

By the end of the second century, the powerful spiritual gifts, including prophecy, which had spread among the first Christians at Pentecost, seem to have disappeared from the church. With the church established and its missionary work well underway, its task is to hand on the gospel teaching. Probably there were always some unorthodox prophets who rolled around like loose cannons, but who were overshadowed by the big names of Ancient Israel or by the spiritual community of the early church. But when the orthodox prophetic voice falls silent once more, these individuals are free to step back into the limelight. And those prophesying the end now have a wealth of biblical detail on which to draw, and a ready-made vocabulary with which to communicate their message.

The rise of the individual

Biblical prophets may come down to us as individuals, but their message is one that is endorsed – at least in theory – by the community from which they emerge. When the Hebrew prophets pointed to the dire consequences of people disobeying God's law, the Israelites believed them. The apocalyptic writers of the last two centuries BC were only giving voice to the widespread belief that the end was near. And Christian prophets who point to Christ's imminent return are doing no more than expressing orthodox religious belief. This remains the case well after Augustine's ban on speculating about the end. Pope Gregory the Great in the sixth century uses dramatic symbolism, but in fact is saying nothing that Christians had not been saying for years.

With the Middle Ages, though, there seems to me to be a distinct change in prophetic direction. From then and right through to the present day there is a certain individuality to many of the prophets of the end. They may well follow the established pattern of calling on people to repent of their wicked ways before the end overtakes them, but they do it in their own distinctive style. Sometimes a prophet will focus on a particular biblical detail and create a whole new emphasis, as we have seen already in the Muggletonians' use of the Two Witnesses prophecy in Revelation. Sometimes it is the forging of a link between biblical prophecy and the prophet's own social circumstances that creates the novelty.

The rise of a new spirituality in the Middle Ages produced mystics who each formulated their own versions of how the human soul progressed to a more intimate knowledge of God. When the mystics turn to prophecy they speak with equally distinctive voices. The twelfth-century German mystic, Hildegard of Bingen, had a series of visions of events at the end of time. She begins one of them with a message that is very much in tune with modern-day ecology movements: 'In the beginning all created things turned green. In the middle period flowers bloomed, but afterward the greening power of life lessened.' This is the familiar idea of the world in decay, but without reference to the declining morality of its peoples. Hildegard's vision here is of the world's life-giving resources gradually drying up as the end approaches.

Later centuries produced prophets whose message was made individual by the place and time at which they lived. Writing on Renaissance England, the American scholar Howard Dobin observes that the English believed that throughout history God revealed the future of their own nation through prophets. He comments: 'The sixteenth-century English prophet came in every variety – contemporary doomsayer, religious fanatic, partisan propagandist, outright fraud.' Today's prophets probably fall into much the same categories, but their messages are highly varied. The ones preaching a religious message do so from all kinds of angles, ingeniously matching biblical end-of-the-world prophecies to people and institutions that range from the former Soviet Union to the World Council of Churches. Secular prophets abound: they may be leaders of oppressed minorities, environmentalists, cosmologists or even flying saucer enthusiasts. In an attempt to demonstrate something of this prophetic individuality in the post-medieval world, I have chosen a few of my favourite characters.

A prophet takes on the state: Girolamo Savonarola

Fifteenth-century Florence saw the rise and fall of an apocalyptic prophet of unusual gifts: he was a powerful preacher, a civic leader and – ultimately – an inspirational martyr. He was a Dominican monk called Girolamo Savonarola who, when he was at his most influential, was prior of the San Marco monastery. Unlike most other prophets his name has lived on, or at least has re-emerged out of the mists of time. In the nineteenth century Savonarola's dream of a united Italy, spiritually and morally reborn, made him the object of a new cult which revered him as a saint, while in England he was a key figure in George Eliot's novel *Romola*.

More than most, Savonarola was a product of his time. His appeal would probably have been much diminished had it not been for the intense atmosphere in which he lived. In the last decades of the fifteenth century Florence was a great centre of Renaissance culture. It was also politically turbulent and vulnerable to outside attack. The Roman Catholic Church had been corrupt for years, since the death of Pope Pius II in 1464, and Italy was a hotbed of conspiracy. What is more, Florence was unusually prone to apocalyptic signs and portents. The city was very conscious of its own greatness. Significantly it had been refounded by Charlemagne, who had given the commune and the surrounding area its independence, and Charles, as we know, had often been seen as a precursor of the end. Various early Renaissance poets depict Florence as the daughter of Rome, yet greater than Rome because of her republican heritage.

Astrology was rife. On 25 November 1484 Jupiter and Saturn were in conjunction, and this was widely believed to be the date on which a great reform in Christian faith would take place. (Historians later noted that Martin Luther may have been born in that month, although whether the year of his birth was 1484 or 1483 is unclear.) Franciscan Spirituals were particularly active at the time, preaching the nearness of the end and the coming of the Angelic Pope. Indeed, speculation about the end had been building up for over a century before Savonarola came on the scene, with frequent predictions of Elijah's return, the coming of Antichrist, and prophecies relating to corruption in the church.

These feelings reached a new pitch in the 1490s, and the death of the Florentine ruler Lorenzo di Medici in 1492 was accompanied by new and ominous signs. By then Savonarola's preaching career was well established and he spoke regularly on a theme that had dominated his thinking since he was a young man: that the church would be scourged and regenerated, and that this would all happen quickly. He supported his views by appealing both to reason and to an allegorical interpretation of the Bible, particularly the Old Testament, and he was convinced that he was inspired by God. Although Savonarola's name was already well known, he attracted particular attention in 1493 when he predicted that the French would invade the following year. 'The only hope that now remains to us,' he declared, 'is that the sword of God may smite the earth.'

The tension was even greater thanks to similar expectations in France, where Charles VIII was seen as a reformer and conqueror of the world. There had been prophecies that he would receive an angelic crown on the Mount of Olives, once he had overcome the infidels of the East. He seemed to be a second Charlemagne, although Savonarola preferred the image of a new Cyrus – a reference to the Persian ruler who conquered Babylonia in 538BC, thereby releasing the Jewish people from their captivity.

Savonarola preached a post-millennialist message: that the Second Coming of Christ would follow the new age of peace which his reforms to church and state would help to bring about. This explains the importance in his thinking of the figure of the Last World Emperor whose actions would bring about the 1,000-year peace, and the idea of the New Jerusalem being set in an earthly city, not a heavenly one. Savonarola interpreted a passage in Zechariah 9, more usually taken to refer to Jesus' entry into Jerusalem on Palm Sunday, as relating to Charles VIII's arrival in Florence: 'Shout aloud, O daughter of Jerusalem! Lo, your king comes to you; triumphant and victorious…' (Zechariah 9:9). He appealed to Daniel to illustrate the need for renewal:

> Daniel the Prophet has said that Antichrist shall come to persecute the Christians in Jerusalem; therefore it is necessary to convert the Turks. And how shall they be converted unless the church be renewed?… Repent ye before the sword be unsheathed, while it be yet unstained with blood; otherwise neither wisdom, power, nor force will avail.

Like Daniel and other apocalyptic prophets Savonarola received visions, and he published a collection of them in 1495 in his *Compendium Revelationum*. On one occasion the vision was of a sword bent towards the earth and two crosses arising from Rome and Jerusalem; in another vision the prophet journeyed to Paradise.

The recurring themes of Savonarola's prophecies were the urgent need for reform in the church, which had been 'made desolate by the corruption of its rulers and the lack of good preachers' (July 1495), and the oppression of his people, which in his early years was put in doom-laden terms:

> The good are oppressed, and the people of Italy become like unto the Egyptians who held God's people in bondage. But already famine, flood, pestilence, and many other signs betoken future ills, and herald the wrath of God.

Both church and state needed to be renewed in readiness for the new age of peace.

In the end Savonarola had to put his prophetic voice to use on his own account. On Ascension Day 1497 he attacked those who denied that he was a prophet, telling the faithful: 'You will be warred against by excommunications, by the sword, and by martyrdom: the days of trial are come.' This prophecy of tribulation before the end came true for the preacher; riots followed his sermon and within a year he died the death of a martyr by burning.

It is clear from historical accounts that Savonarola was an important figure in the political life of Florence at the time, as well as an inspired preacher of reform and a millennial prophet. In his prophecy all the complex circumstances of his day join with the rich tradition of apocalyptic signs, figures and rhetoric. In her novel George Eliot passed judgment on his wide-ranging appeal: 'In Savonarola's preaching there were strains that appealed to the very finest susceptibilities of men's natures, and there were elements that gratified low egoism, tickled gossiping curiosity, and fascinated timorous superstition.'

Three women prophets

The Yorkshire prophetess

> The world shall end when the High
> Bridge is thrice fallen.

The bridge in question carries the busy A59 across the river Nidd on the outskirts of the Yorkshire town of Knaresborough. It has already fallen twice in its long history, and for those disposed to wait for its third collapse in comfort, 'The World's End' public house is conveniently placed alongside it.

Knaresborough was the home of Mother Shipton, one of Britain's best known sixteenth-century women prophets. The town has made the most of its asset and there is an impressive visitors' centre around the cave where she is said to have been born, on a spectacularly beautiful river site. Mother Shipton was born in 1488, three years after the end of the Wars of the Roses. She was the illegitimate daughter of a local girl and was given the name Ursula. The cave where her young mother chose to give birth is a strange place. It backs onto an ancient well which was renowned as a place of evil, probably because the high mineral content of the waterfall that runs into it causes anything in its path to become petrified. For centuries people have hung objects in the path of the cascading water and returned after a few weeks to find them turned to stone. Today the nearby giftshop sells small teddy bears for that same purpose.

To be born so close to the Petrifying Well would probably have been enough in the fifteenth century for the child to be regarded with a certain amount of fear. Any such susperstition was no doubt compounded by a thunderstorm on the night of Ursula's birth and by her physical appearance: her face was apparently so ugly that she was regarded as deformed and said to be the devil's child. But despite all these disadvantages she was married at the age of twenty-four to the local carpenter, Toby Shipton, and seems to have enjoyed a happy, if childless, marriage.

Ursula Shipton's fame seems to have begun at a purely local level when she began to acquire a reputation for predictions of a largely commonsensical nature. But Knaresborough is less than twenty miles from the city of York, and a good few notable figures of the time were coming and going through Mother Shipton's part of the world and were no doubt the subject of much local gossip. The most famous was Cardinal Thomas Wolsey, the Lord Chancellor of England, who inflicted heavy taxes on rich and poor alike, and who effectively ruled the country while the King was engaged in the Thirty Years War with France. Wolsey had already embarked on his policy of dissolving the monasteries, and one of Mother Shipton's visitors was the Abbot of Beverly who perhaps feared for his own minster. In any event it was to him that Mother Shipton delivered certain prophecies relating to national leaders and events; and although they were mainly in images they were not hard to interpret. A notable prophecy was that Cardinal Wolsey, although Archbishop of York, would never reach the city alive, and so it proved.

Ursula Shipton died in 1561 and her long life spanned many significant events in English history. Although much of what she prophesied clearly related to contemporary events, her penchant for imagery allowed subsequent generations to reinterpret her prophecies in terms of their own time.

Her imagery intermingles biblical language and some ideas peculiar to her own day. In foretelling peace she uses the Old Testament prophecy of swords being turned into ploughshares (Joel 3:10), only to follow it with an image of war – possibly even the final battle – which draws on biblical apocalyptic imagery:

> The fiery year as soon as o'er,
> Peace shall then be as before;
> Plenty everywhere be found,
> And men with swords shall plough the ground.
> The time shall come when seas of blood
> Shall mingle with a greater flood.
> Carriages without horses shall go.
> And accidents fill the world with woe.

Some modern commentators have claimed that these lines prophesy motor vehicles. What is of course much more likely is that the carriages without horses are an image of the world in chaos; indeed Mother Shipton makes that explicit a few lines later:

> The world upside down shall be
> And gold found at the root of a tree.

It is very likely that these verses are a later reworking of Mother Shipton's originals, since an edition of her prophecies published in 1797 is described as being 'compiled from the Original Scarce Editions and Corrected by S. Baker'. The extent of these 'corrections' is impossible to gauge. The publisher notes that the original is so scarce that it 'has been frequently sold for Five Shillings!!!' – a princely sum in those days. This in itself is significant since it suggests that later centuries saw in the prophecies a relevance for their own time.

Apart from the comment on Knaresborough bridge – of which the rational interpretation might be that it was a warning about the manifest lack of safety – Mother Shipton has nothing explicit to say about the end of the world. Yet for a period such as hers, where other prophets, perhaps due to the turmoil of the time, were prophesying the end, it cannot be ruled out that people understood what she had to say in such terms. Certainly she was not forgotten. A century later the Plague and the Great Fire of London, both seen by some as signs of the end, were taken to be fulfilling her prophecies.

In Mother Shipton's sayings a number of features combine. Throughout her life she was the focus of popular superstition and genuine fear in the light of her association with a then inexplicable phenomenon of nature. The period in which she lived was one of considerable social upheaval; and with the printed word still barely a factor to be taken into account, rumours spread easily. What little we know of Mother Shipton's character suggests an intelligence that was able to combine commonsense prediction with prophecy that used words and images from biblical apocalyptic and put them in the form of popular verse. Above all, it was a language sufficiently general and figurative to ensure that the prophecies would bear constant reinterpretation by future generations living in similarly uncertain times. Her eighteenth-century publisher pays tribute to the respect given to this ordinary, yet pious woman throughout most of her adult life:

> She was supernaturally endowed with an uncommon Penetration into Things, for which she became so famous, in time, that great numbers of all ranks and degrees resorted to her Habitation to hear her Wonderful Discourses.

The English aristocrat: 'Never so mad a ladie'

The year was 1633. The place: the Court of High Arches. This was the provincial court of the Archbishop of Canterbury and was so called because it was at St Mary-le-Bow which was built on arches. As the Court of Arches it still survives today, hearing appeals from judgments of consistory courts (the Church of England's own courts). In the seventeenth century it was a court of first instance in all ecclesiastical matters and a court of appeal from all diocesan courts within the Province of Canterbury.

On a day in October 1633 the Dean of Arches was doodling as he listened to the case being heard before him. The person on trial was a well-educated lady of noble birth. Her name was Lady Eleanor Douglas, and by changing her title from Lady to Dame and using her maiden name of Audeley the Dean came up with an anagram: 'Never so mad a ladie.' It was an appropriate sentiment; if Lady Eleanor was at that stage only 'mad' insofar as she acted in a way atypical of her sex, by the end of her life she was decidedly odd.

The charge which was read to Lady Eleanor on 8 October was for selling her books in England 'contrary to the Decree of Star Chamber', the infamous court which dealt especially with perceived public order offences. These books were alleged to contain 'scandalous matter' relating to persons whose names appeared in anagrams and included a prediction that Charles I, whom Eleanor likened to Belshazzar, would meet a violent end. There was specific mention of Lady Eleanor's 'Exposition of divers parts... of the Prophet Daniel, some other scandalous matter by way of Anagram or otherwise, against Ecclesiastical persons and Judges of eminent place... Forasmuch as she took upon her (which much unbeseemed her sex) not only to interpret the scriptures... but also to be a Prophetess...'. Three weeks later Lady Eleanor was fined £3,000 and imprisoned in the Tower Gatehouse, where she remained for two years before her daughter managed to get her released. Yet even then she was barely at the beginning of her prophetic career.

Eleanor Douglas was the youngest daughter of Baron Audeley, a Fellow of Magdalen College, Oxford. In 1609 she married Sir John Davies, the Attorney-General for Ireland. The events that brought her to wider public attention began in 1625 when she 'heard early in the morning a Voice from Heaven, speaking as through a Trumpet these words: There is Nineteen years and a half to the Judgment Day.' This was followed by a couple of unnervingly accurate predictions: the death of her husband within three years (he died in December 1626) and the death of the Duke of Buckingham (who was assassinated in 1628). Meanwhile Eleanor had married again; her new husband was Sir Archibald Douglas who, like her first husband, burned her writings. Douglas went mad and died in 1644. After her imprisonment Eleanor stepped up her activities and was again sent to the Tower. After her release in 1640 she published a succession of pamphlets right up to her death in 1652, when she was buried alongside her first husband at St Martins in the Fields in London.

Only one of Eleanor's works was published legally: her *Strange and Wonderful Prophecies*, which described how her prophecies had been fulfilled since she had been called to follow in the footsteps of the prophet Daniel some fourteen years earlier. The rest were all banned and published privately, and were mainly on apocalyptic themes, including the Second Coming which she predicted would happen in 1700, and various biblical prophecies.

Eleanor's pamphlets cannot in all honesty be said to be either clearly or sensibly written; even so, they reflect something of her time as well as her mind. At the beginning of her 1644 publication on Daniel 7, Eleanor follows prophetic convention in claiming special insight into the meaning of the text, referring to the 'mistery for this time reserved, hitherto with the Kingdome of Heavens great seale shut up'. More significantly, this revelation is especially kept for the people of her own country. Some tortuous arguments lead her finally to exclaim: 'O Daniel greatly beloved man, as much to say too, O King of great Britaine!' *The Restitution of Prophecy* (printed in 1651) draws on heraldry and astrology in order to situate the events of Revelation 17 in Eleanor's own time and country. Although the style is rambling and sometimes incoherent, Eleanor's conviction that she is living in the last days is unmistakable.

Unlike some women of a lower social class, there is no evidence that Lady Eleanor Davies commanded any respect as a prophet. Quite the reverse: she was clearly a nuisance to secular and religious authorities alike and a great embarrassment to her long-suffering family. She became obsessed with biblical symbolism to the extent that she saw apocalyptic significance in the horns on the coats of arms of Derby and Oxford. Possibly she was deranged, but her wealth enabled her to publish her ramblings privately. Nonetheless, her obsession was also an obsession of her time, and her conviction that the Lord would return to the English was equally a conviction held by many in the turbulent 1640s. Today the crypt of St Martins where Eleanor is buried has no complete record of who lies there. It is a noisy tourist attraction where visitors to central London can buy food and souvenirs – Lady Eleanor's resting place is as turbulent as she was herself in life.

Joanna Southcott and 'The Sealed of the Lord'

The village of Gittisham (near the Devonshire market town of Honiton) is tucked away down a country lane that leads off the A303, once the only road link between Salisbury and Exeter. The nearby village of Ottery St Mary has a certain claim to fame, as the birthplace of the poet Coleridge in 1772. But, if it wishes, Gittisham can boast its own prophet – Joanna Southcott, daughter of a local farmer, who was born there in 1750.

In the course of her life Joanna wrote no fewer than sixty-five books and pamphlets which she maintained were dictated to her by the Spirit. The verdict of one of her critics, one Dr Hughson, was that they were 'the witless efflorescences of a distracted old woman' (Joanna was sixty-four when she died). She had a marked obsession with the devil, but unlike perhaps the majority of prophets she remained conscious of the possibility that she might be mistaken, a false prophet, and she brought to the millenarian activities of the 1800s a message which drew on a particular aspect of the book of Revelation: the sealing of the people of God.

Joanna's first recorded spiritual experience happened when she was just fifteen. It was an exorcism which she performed for a dying neighbour who thought he had seen the devil. When she was twenty-one, Joanna moved to Exeter where she worked for an upholsterer and came into contact with the teaching of John Wesley. Nothing more is heard of her for another twenty-one years when – in the tradition of Mother Shipton – she attracted attention by accurately prophesying the death of the Bishop of Exeter. This seems to have been the first instance of her 'sealed' prophecies – predictions which were written down and sealed up until such time as anyone cared to break the seal and check their accuracy.

In 1801 Joanna published her first book, entitled *Strange Effects of Faith*. Gathering a small following, mainly women, she began her travels to London and the North of England, proclaiming that the Second Coming was imminent. At the same time she distributed more sealed prophecies, which had to do with national and international events, and constantly urged her listeners to check her credibility.

Joanna's need to prove her authenticity was a purely practical one. The people who were initially responsible for promoting her and financing her trip to London were the followers of Richard Brothers. Brothers too believed that the end was near and had a similar preoccupation with the devil. The problem was that he was obviously deranged, even in the eyes of a public who were famously tolerant of religious oddballs. In 1795 Brothers had published a two-volume work entitled *A Revealed Knowledge of the Prophecies and Times*, convinced that his role was to gather up the dispersed Jews and lead them to Palestine. This was not in itself an unusual idea at the time, but Brothers spent thirty years of his life not only planning a New

Jerusalem, but designing its flags, uniforms and palaces. Following a hostile article in *The Times* in March 1795, which sarcastically dubbed him 'the Great Prophet of Paddington Street', Brothers was arrested, declared insane and shut up in a madhouse until 1806. On his release he published a book in which he claimed to be the Messiah. Three years before this Joanna Southcott had prophesied destruction if Brothers was not freed, and now she tried to help him again by publishing an *Answer to Mr Brothers' Book*, which argued that Brothers had been misled by a bad spirit. After that little more is heard of him until his death in 1825, although his followers continued to study the Bible and to support Joanna in his place.

Seals are used in two ways in Revelation. In chapter 5 John has a vision of a scroll sealed with seven seals which are opened in turn in chapter 6 to release a series of disasters on the earth. Intentionally or not, Joanna echoes this with her sealed prophecies (she used a seal bearing the initials J.C. which she appropriated from her work at the haberdashers). The other use of seals is to mark or brand people: in Revelation 7, an angel puts a protective mark (or 'seal') on 144,000 people, that is 12,000 from each of the twelve tribes of Israel before the full force of destruction is let loose upon the earth. And it is this activity of sealing that Joanna characteristically undertook.

'Sealing up the people' began in Leeds in 1803 when Joanna promised that the seals would offer divine protection against the enemy Napoleon Bonaparte, who, she said, would not harm England until the sealing was finished. Joanna's opponents argued that she kept her 20,000 'sealed people' fearful, feeding them stories of disasters that had afflicted other nations. The 'sealed' would not only overpower Napoleon if he invaded: they would work miracles and convert the world, having first made England 'a happy land'.

At the same time Joanna was prophesying that the 1,000-year reign of Christ would begin in 1807, preceded by judgment in the three years before it. In a series of 'warnings to the world', Joanna predicted sickness, wars and shipwrecks and the gathering in of the Jews. The 'unerring Spirit of God' proclaimed: 'Men may mourn like the rain, or roar like the winds, and say, the harvest is over: the day is ended, and we are not saved: for I shall cut short the harvest, if I do not destroy it; and I shall cut short the land also.'

When the years in question had passed, Joanna reformulated her prophecies. Judgment was now to begin at the start of 1809 in the 'House of God'. One of her critics commented unkindly, 'It cannot be said that the judgments last winter began at the House of God, unless it can be proved that Covent Garden, or Drury Lane Theatre, was the House of God; both of which were burnt about that time.'

Joanna's life ended in delusion and disappointment. In 1813 she became convinced that she was to give birth to the second Messiah, and indeed there seems to have been evidence of a hysterical pregnancy that lasted many months. She died at the close of the year in 1814, having inspired the poet William Blake to write a four-line epigram entitled 'On the Virginity of the Virgin Mary and Johanna Southcott':

> Whate'er is done to her she cannot know,
> And if you'll ask her she will swear it so.
> Whether 'tis good or evil none's to blame:
> No one can take the pride, no one the shame.

Prophecy and legend

There is an old legend of a first-century Jew whom Christ condemned to wander the earth until he returned. I came across his story one evening in Oxford's Bodleian library when I was looking through a collection of early nineteenth-century pamphlets. It was in a tiny eight-page publication entitled *The Wandering Jew; or The Shoemaker of Jerusalem. Who lived when our Lord and Saviour Jesus Christ was crucified and by Him appointed to wander until He comes again*. According to this version of the legend, Jesus stopped to rest at a shoemaker's stall on his way to the cross. But the shoemaker spat at him and drove him away, to which Jesus responded: 'For this thing thou shalt never rest, but wander till I come again upon the earth'.

What was remarkable about this particular pamphlet was how the story continued. My attention was caught in the first place by an addition to the main title, which ran: 'With His Travels, Method of Living, and a Discourse with some Clergymen about the End of the World'. According to the author, the Wandering Jew had travelled across Asia, Africa and America, 'and is now on his journey to visit every town in Europe'. At this point the old legend is tied in with some strange contemporary goings-on in the city of Hull, where the 'Wandering Jew' sought accommodation. Because of his unsavoury appearance, his landlord, one Dr Hall, locked him in his room; but the next morning the citizens found the door open, although the Jew had made no attempt to escape. The Jew offered to be put in chains, and when the doctor complied the chains fell off him: 'human force cannot confine him whom the Almighty had sentenced to want a resting place.' They painted his picture and concluded that he looked neither old nor young, but just as he was when his journey began 1,769 years before.

There were plenty of strange stories about, it seems, in the early 1800s. But what struck me about this one was that the figure of the Wandering Jew is taken up and used as a prophet of the end to the people of Hull. In other words, the writer of the pamphlet is behaving just like the authors of apocalyptic books 2,000 years before: he takes a legendary figure and uses him as a mouthpiece for eschatological prophecy.

The story went on like this. Four ministers from Hull questioned the Jew: 'Can you tell how long Moses and the Prophets prophesied the world would stand?' The answer is not unfamiliar: the world would last 6,000 years, and this time is divided into three equal periods: from creation to the flood, from the flood to Christ and from Christ to the present (which is apparently AD1769). The writer concludes: 'There cannot be many more than 200 years to come to the time prophesied for the world to be at an end; but the exact time is not known, [Christ] said it is not known to the angels in heaven.' Then comes the prophecy that first the Jewish people will return to Jerusalem:

> And he prophesies, that before the end of the world the Jews shall be gathered together from all parts of the world, and return to Jerusalem, and live there, and it shall flourish as much as ever; and that they, and all others, shall become Christians, that wars shall cease, and the whole world live in unity with one another.

The four clerics put a further question to the Jew, as to why people's lives are now shorter than they were in Old Testament times. His answer takes up another familiar theme:

> And as the world declines, so does the nature of men and women; and all creatures therein; but as the world gets shorter and shorter, so shall the life of men, even as a span long.

The world is in decline, the end is not far off, but first the Jews must be gathered up and converted. These are straightforward, familiar eschatological prophecies. The novelty of the North Yorkshire ministers whose names appear at the end of the pamphlet is to put them in the mouth of a legendary character, and, given his nature, this perhaps gives special weight to the prophecy about the Jews. So they conclude that it is 'convenient to publish it, for the good of all Christians'.

'Mrs Keech' and the prophecy from outer space

In 1956 three sociologists published a study of human behaviour called *When Prophecy Fails*. Their aim was to demonstrate how people respond when a belief to which they are deeply committed is shown to be false beyond all possible doubt. What they found was that far from retreating from their position when their belief is 'disconfirmed', such believers demonstrate even greater fervour than before. To some extent this was already known from the eschatological prophets of history. The sixteenth-century Anabaptists who expected the millennium in 1533 were preaching with renewed enthusiasm a year later. A Jewish sect who believed that the Messiah would come in 1648 readily accepted a Christian date of 1666 instead when he failed to materialize.

Festinger and his colleagues offer a fascinating analysis of such behaviour, which includes a list of five conditions which must obtain if the belief is to persist. Apart from deep commitment, the believer must, for example, have taken some important action 'that is difficult to undo', and must also have support from other believers: an isolated believer is unlikely to be able to withstand the evidence against the prophecy. What is even more fascinating, though, is the particular case study they present. All the names and places, and even the year in question, are disguised; all that can be deduced is that the events took place somewhere in the United States, probably in the early 1950s.

'Mrs Keech' claimed to be a prophetic intermediary. She received and wrote down messages from spiritual beings in outer space. The essence of her prophecy was that on 21 December (the year is unspecified) the world would be largely wiped out by a flood whose waters would extend from the Arctic to the Gulf of Mexico. Those chosen to survive would be rescued by flying saucers.

The language of Mrs Keech's revelations owes more than a little to traditional Christian apocalyptic, although her religious view is a dualistic one: the forces of light are pitted against the prince of darkness. The 'age of darkness' and worldwide upheaval was at hand, but on 15 August she wrote:

> When the resurrected have been resurrected or taken up – it will be as a great burst of light… the ground in the earth to a depth of thirty feet will be bright… for the earth will be purified. In the midst of this it is to be recorded that a great wave rushes into the rocky mountains… The slopes of the side to the east will be the beginning of a new civilization upon which will be the new order, in the light…

The sociologists pursued their research by infiltrating observers into the small band of believers that gathered round Mrs Keech and her associate 'Dr Armstrong'. Believers were encouraged to give up their jobs and to wait for further orders from space. Although they had released their message to the world in September, it had had little effect, and in the months that followed the group's behaviour became increasingly secretive.

There was also division within the group. Mrs Keech denied that the world would end on 21 December, but Dr Armstrong – by now sacked from his college teaching post – countered with a prophecy of his own:

> The Supreme Being is going to clean house by sinking all of the land masses as we know them now and raising the land masses now under the sea. There will be a washing of the world with water. Some will be saved by being taken off the earth in space craft.

Guided by their prophets the believers prepared to be taken off the planet in the days before the expected end. Their preparations included removing all metal (such as zips) from their clothing, so that they could enter the saucers without danger, even if their trousers were held up with string. When the vital date passed the group suddenly went public: the prophets sought media attention and used the failure of their prophecies as an excuse to reaffirm their beliefs to a wider audience.

Statistically, Mrs Keech seems to have been quite successful as a prophet. Of the eleven members in the group, only two gave up their belief in her writings, while two more expressed doubts. Five were unshaken in their faith and two ended up more strongly convinced than before. The group did not make any serious attempt to impose their beliefs on other people – their philosophy was that 'those who are ready will be sent'. Even so, everything came to an abrupt end, when on 26 December the leaders were charged with disturbing the peace and contributing to the delinquency of minors, and it was not long before the threat of legal action dispersed the group. The anonymous 'Mrs Keech' seems to have disappeared from the prophetic scene as suddenly as she arrived – unless, of course, she has since returned in another guise.

Prophets have always been catalysts for action. Without them expectations of the end would be unfocused and incoherent. Professor K. Burridge, who has investigated millennialism from an anthropological viewpoint, has defined a prophet as someone who 'organizes the new assumptions and articulates them; who is listened to and found acceptable; whose revelation is accorded authority for however brief a period'. And each of the prophets I have described meets these criteria, at least within their own limited circles. Burridge also comments on women prophets: 'Besides being prophets in the ordinary sense they also participate in an infrastructure of competition and privilege, that of men versus women in a world where men are privileged.' This I find less convincing. There is, I think, a sense in which women are felt (by men and women alike) to be more sensitive to prophetic promptings, more 'religious'; when world-threatening matters are at stake it seems that men have had little hesitation in listening to women prophets and supporting them, without necessarily feeling threatened.

All end-of-the-world prophets so far have been doomed to fail. But they have made a special contribution to the religious and cultural life of their time. They have created a synthesis of the particular concerns of their day and the more general age-old prophetic traditions. Some of the special interpretations they have introduced into eschatology will be the subject-matter of chapter 9.

References

K. Burridge, *New Heaven, New Earth*, Blackwell, Oxford, 1971.

Howard Dobin, *Merlin's Disciples: Prophecy, Poetry, and Power in Renaissance England*, Stanford University Press, 1990.

George Eliot, *Romola*, 1862–3; World's Classics series, Oxford University Press, 1994.

L. Festinger, H.W. Riecken and S. Schachter, *When Prophecy Fails*, University of Minnesota Press, 1956.

Hildegard of Bingen, *Book of Divine Works*, edited by M. Fox, Santa Fe, Bear & Co. Inc., 1987.

Pasquale Villari, *Life and Times of Girolamo Savonarola*, London, Fisher Unwin, 1888.

Donald Weinstein, *Savonarola and Florence: Prophecy and Patriotism in the Renaissance*, Princeton, NJ, Princeton University Press, 1970.

Chapter 8

The Drama of the End

'A black sun arose: an orb the size of that luminary, but dark, defined, whose beams were shadows, ascended from the west; in about an hour it had reached the meridian and eclipsed the bright parent of day.'

Mary Shelley, *The Last Man*

Today Mary Shelley is best remembered as the author of *Frankenstein*, the Gothic novel of 1818 which has been repeatedly distorted and popularized on film since the early days of the cinema. Decidedly less popular is the book she wrote seven years later called *The Last Man*. There are certain similarities between the two: both stories have a first-person narrator and both involve epic journeys across Europe. Both narrators are engaged in a hopeless pursuit: the one in a futile search for his horrific monster, the other endlessly seeking refuge from a plague which decimates whole nations.

The Last Man is one of a number of works representing what some literary critics term 'romantic apocalypse'. Like some of William Blake's poems, Mary Shelley's novel shows us people caught up in the end of history. Of course, as the critic Steven Goldsmith has pointed out, this is an impossible situation: logically there cannot be a physical book describing the end. Even St John's Revelation was no more than a vision. In literary terms, this must be the ultimate way in which the romantic hero is set apart from his fellow human beings, as the last inhabitant of their world. But, in the tradition of apocalyptic writing, *The Last Man* and texts like it have a different place altogether. They are part of a long tradition of creating drama out of the signs, people and events of the end. Such compositions, whether in art or literature, vary in form according to the culture of their time. So the themes of the early Jewish and Christian apocalypses are expanded and developed through medieval mystery plays to contemporary science fiction, and from the thirteenth-century illustrators of the book of Revelation and the sculptors of our great cathedrals, to artists' visions of apocalypse inspired by the horrors of modern warfare.

Mary Shelley's prose style does not make for easy reading, but her novel seems to have it all, at least as far as the events leading up to the end are concerned. The story is set at the end of the twenty-first century, when Britain is a republic and people travel round by balloon. The time, near the beginning of the third millennium, may be significant, since the early chapters describe a period of peace in which the arts flourish and the main characters are content – a millennial-type interlude which might have been a preliminary to an earthly paradise. But the irresistible spread of plague brings portents of disaster: the black sun (reminiscent of Revelation 6:12), the appearance of the moon, stars and night animals in daytime, and the terror of wild beasts. The natural world becomes threatening – 'Nature… had turned on us a brow of menace' – as storms, plague and famine wreak havoc. Prophets appear who reduce some of the population to physical wrecks: 'Weak-spirited women died of fear… men of robust form and seeming strength fell into idiocy and madness, racked by the dread of coming eternity.' As a result of all this, morality collapses as people begin to live only for the present.

One particular characteristic of Mary Shelley's time that finds expression in the book is the expectation that the English should receive special treatment. The narrator and his family fleeing the plague are described – with heavy biblical overtones – as 'the numbered remnant of the English nation'. Even this cannot save them, though, and the chaos worsens with the appearance of three new suns to orbit our own sun, and with crazed horses and cattle plunging into the sea. The last man remains alone in 'a voiceless empty world'.

Developments like this are only possible thanks to the drama inherent in even the earliest visions of the end of time. From an early date too, poets used events of the end to enliven their narratives of wholly secular events. A good example of this is in the oldest surviving work of literature in medieval French, the *Song of Roland*. Composed around 1100, it tells the story of Roland, nephew of the Emperor Charlemagne, who died a hero's death in a battle against the Saracens in the Spanish Pyrenees in the year 778. Roland's death is brought about by a traitor in his own side, and as his end approaches, the story is filled with portents of the end of the age:

143

Back in France there was a great storm
With tempest, thunder and wind,
Rain and hail fell beyond measure
Thunderbolts struck repeatedly,
And the earth shook…
At midday there was thick darkness,
There was no light except flashes of lightning,
There was no one who was not greatly afraid.
Many said: 'This is without doubt the end of the age.'

The allusion to the darkness that covered the earth at midday as at the time of Christ's crucifixion simply increases the drama, and the medieval audience could hardly fail to be struck with terror themselves as their hero's death is described in terms of the signs of the end. These bring their own weight to bear on the wider significance of Roland's death: the age of the great Emperor Charles is seen as nearing its end – nothing will be the same again.

Plays on the end

In the early Middle Ages in Western Europe religion and secular life were virtually inseparable in the arts as well as in everyday affairs, and Christian symbols were easily recognized and widely employed. Not surprisingly, the earliest literature makes extensive use of the language and symbolism associated with the last things. Sometimes this is obviously because of the subject matter, which might take the form of events on the Day of Judgment or the life of Antichrist; sometimes it is simply that writers enlist the help of those well-known symbols to enliven the presentation of dramatic events of their own creation.

The medieval mystery plays are the oldest literary forms to portray scenes of the Last Judgment. These plays sprang out of the liturgy of the church, which specified particular (Latin) Bible readings according to the season of the church's year. By the twelfth century the great stories associated particularly with Easter and Pentecost were being acted out of doors in the language of the ordinary people. Gradually they acquired extra non-biblical features to keep the audience amused and interested – little devils and their antics, representing hell, were one such popular diversion.

The earliest surviving text of a mystery play is the Anglo-Norman *Mystère d'Adam* (the 'Adam' play) which dates from the twelfth century. It begins at creation and moves through Adam and Eve in the Garden of Eden and the Fall, to the drama of Cain and Abel, and ends with a procession of Old Testament prophets who look forward to the birth of Christ and the redemption of the world. Sadly the original ending of the play has been lost, but it may well have gone on to include an account of Christ's Second Coming. In any case it was not long before one of the scribes responsible for making a copy of the Adam play replaced the final scene with something from a completely different tradition: the 'Fifteen Signs of Judgment'.

Like the early mystery plays the various versions of the 'Fifteen Signs' are a popular verse form which derives from something more specialized. The texts are found in a variety of Western European languages, ranging from Frisian and Flemish, Irish, Welsh and Basque, to the emerging 'national' languages of English, French, Spanish and Italian. Their exact literary origin is uncertain, although one possibility is that they stem from the fifth-century *Apocalypse of Thomas*, while some versions claim that they derive from the fourth-century writings of Jerome. Whatever their origin, though, the Fifteen Signs were always a literary form. Unlike the 'signs' that feature in Old Testament prophecies and in the gospels and were accepted as biblical tradition, these fifteen (or in some texts seven) signs were seen as legendary and were never held to be a matter of faith.

The widespread diffusion of this form, both in space and time (they cover a period of 800 years), suggests an enduring popularity. The signs are alluded to in art, in the fifteenth-century Books of Hours, in stained glass and in tapestries in France and in German woodcuts. Yet this raises more questions than it answers. Why, for instance, fifteen signs?

The legend is that one sign is revealed on each of the fifteen days before doomsday. The significance of the number has never been satisfactorily established, although it is a popular one in medieval literature, which has the 'Fifteen Joys of the Virgin' and the 'Fifteen Sermons of Christ', as well as a secular counterpart, the 'Fifteen Joys of Marriage'. Apart from an unlikely allusion to the fifteen cubit measurement for Noah's ark in Genesis there is no obvious biblical parallel. But the answer may be simpler than that. It is a French convention to reckon a fortnight as fifteen days (rather than fourteen as in English). If the signs were to last two weeks, it might be reasonable to assume that a third week (which gives a perfect number) was either devoted to judgment itself or was a time of peace inaugurated by judgment on the fifteenth day. This would tie in with the ending of the best-known French version in which the earth and sky are completely burnt up on the fifteenth day, and God makes a new heaven and a new earth. We can then assume that other literary forms based on fifteen units are natural spin-offs from the original.

Where the purpose of the work is stated it is a moralizing one. The French poet begins on a familiar note by deploring how bad things are getting, with widespread wrongdoing and a general falling away from faith. He predicts that there will be universal sorrow and grievous judgment 'when this age ends', which will lead to happiness for the good. The poet claims his authority from various Old Testament figures – prophets, patriarchs and kings.

What, though, of the signs themselves? From biblical and apocryphal writings alone, one would be hard pressed to come up with fifteen different portents of the end. The beauty of this popular form, though, is that these 'basic' biblical signs are richly augmented with ideas that must reflect people's imaginations at work on ancient prophecies and supplementing them with their own hopes and fears; in this way events can be included which originally had little or no association with the end.

The fifteen days are mostly marked by groups of signs. Day One sees the sky raining blood, which colours the whole earth. On this day too unborn children cry out to God from their mothers' wombs, pleading not to be born but to remain 'nothing'. Already we can see the poet's imagination in action: inspired by the detail of blood in Joel, he adds the detail of the whole earth being affected by it and its colour changing. The tradition of babies crying out from the womb is not originally an apocalyptic symbol; it is used, for example, by the Psalmist, while the gospels tell us of the emotion of an unborn child (John the Baptist leaped for joy when his mother met Mary).

This sign is different from the moon turning to blood, which does not happen until Day Four, following the loss of light once the stars have fallen into the abyss (Day Two) and the sun has been blotted out (Day Three). There may seem to be some logical sequence to these first days, but thereafter events pile up virtually at random: the animals fall mutely into great chasms, war breaks out, and, in an episode reminiscent of the Israelites crossing the Red Sea, the sea rises to the sky driving the fish to seek refuge in the earth. On Day Eleven winds from all quarters pull the newly dead from their graves, blowing them up into the sky to mingle with devils.

The language is doom-laden and dramatic, as each day is worse than the last, until the trumpets sound for the Day of Judgment and the fate of the judged is described in a gentler tone. The writer laments the fate of those consigned to hell and ends with a prayer for the living, that they may be included among the righteous:

> Help us in this, holy Mary
> Amen, amen, let each reply.

This pattern of a more or less extravagant description of the end, with some appeal to biblical texts, followed by a prayer for salvation, or at least for improvement, becomes a common one. A thirteenth-century English poem called 'Doomsday' (already quoted in chapter 4) is a much more succinct example. It begins with the poet expressing his fear: 'When I think on Doomsday I am full sore afraid', and then mentions only the all-consuming fire that shall come one Saturday night (presumably the significance is that the following day is the day of resurrection) and the angels heralding Judgment Day. Human beings are depicted as helpless before God; Christ addresses the righteous and the sinners, and the final verse is again a prayer to Mary, 'That she our souls into the kingdom of heaven bring'. In all the surviving manuscripts this poem is followed by another, 'The Latemost Day', which ends with an exhortation to godly living.

A century later, literary portents of the end become real events and, as we have seen, these were incorporated into religious poetry with strong apocalyptic overtones ('Verses on the Earthquake of 1382', page 82 above). This, though, does not prevent Chaucer alluding to portents of the end to comic effect in 'The Miller's Tale', in which the wily Nicholas devises an elaborate plot to deceive the local carpenter, with the aim of seducing his wife:

> I have found out, through my astrology,
> By gazing in the moon, that's shining bright,
> That on Monday next at about nine at night,
> There'll be a fall of rain – so fierce in spate
> Even Noah's flood was never so great.
> 'This world', said he, 'in less time than an hour
> Must all be drowned, so frightful the downpour.
> Thus all mankind must drown and wholly perish.'

Staging the end

Signs of the end may make great reading, but they do not work well on stage. The real dramas of the end sprang out of the mystery play tradition, the earliest being a twelfth-century German work called the *Ludus Paschalis de Anti-Christo* ('The Easter Play of Antichrist'). Although based on events in Revelation, it is also said to contain an echo of quarrels between the German emperor, Frederick Barbarossa (whom we have already encountered as a possible Last World Emperor), and Pope Alexander III.

Although the Last Judgment had been represented in art in Eastern and Western Christendom since a very early date, it does not appear in any developed way on stage until the fourteenth century. This may be because of the technical requirements of such an undertaking, since scenes need to be set not only alongside each other but on top of one another, as events move between earth and heaven or heaven and hell.

This is certainly the setting demanded by the late fourteenth-century French play, *Le Jour du Jugement* ('Judgment Day'). Unlike its German predecessor, it is not a straight liturgical play, but a full-blown drama that draws on events in Revelation and a variety of contemporary legends and preoccupations as well. The scene is set in a lengthy prologue in which a preacher tells of the miseries to come, the signs of the end, and the appearance of Enoch, Elijah and Antichrist. We then see Satan with a multitude of devils, before the mother of Antichrist appears. She asserts that she is Jewish and hates all Christians, although before her child is born she pledges allegiance to Muhammad, and later in the play there is a suggestion that Antichrist is in fact Egyptian. As the play develops extra details are introduced. Coins are struck bearing the image of Antichrist; a wicked bishop hails him as his lord; and when Antichrist succeeds in bringing a corpse back to life he is greeted as 'true God, full of grace!'.

Later in the play the action switches to heaven. St John tells us that the earth has been burnt up and the world destroyed, whereupon God sends the four gospel-writers to the four corners of the globe to raise the dead. When the judgment begins, typical religious and secular leaders make their appearance. The damned include a lawyer, a bailiff, an abbess, and a usurer who is the object of God's special condemnation in that his wife, servant and child are all damned with him. When it comes to the judgment of the righteous, the characters act out the words of Christ in Matthew 25. God says: 'I was hungry and you gave me food, I was thirsty and you gave me drink...' and so on, and the just reply: 'When did we see thee hungry and feed thee, or thirsty and gave thee drink?' Meanwhile, down below, the lawyer is seeking leave to appeal against his sentence.

The judgment play has, if not a cast of thousands, then at least enough parts to keep a small community busy, and it is reckoned to have taken two to three hours to perform. There are allusions to some of the theological and political issues of the day, including the great schism with its rival papacies in Rome and Avignon. The treatment of the usurer is harsher than orthodox theology required, and this may reflect popular thinking of the time. Indeed, before the fourteenth century there were no children or elderly people to be seen in representations of the Last Judgment: the dead seem to have been resurrected as thirty-year-old adults. The French play is also notably anti-Semitic, perhaps in response to the expulsions of Jews from France under Charles VI. However, the play is perhaps most striking for its central character of Antichrist, a figure of great interest to the faithful at the time, although the Lateran Council in 1516 was to impose a clamp-down on over-precise prophecies relating to both Antichrist and the Last Judgment.

This type of drama did not last very long. It came late to the Middle Ages and was soon superseded by Renaissance concerns. Probably once the action was fully worked out there was not much more to be done with it. Certainly, a fifteenth-century version from Provence has already introduced a strong allegorical note into the judgment scene, where personified vices such as Pride and Gluttony are put on trial rather than typical human characters. Even so, as stage representations of the biblical and post-biblical events of the end, these plays are as rich in drama as the constraints of the time allow.

The vision of William Blake

Few artists can have dramatized popular thinking on the end quite so comprehensively as the eighteenth-century artist and poet William Blake. And Blake does much more than simply depict the events of the end in his art and his poems. He brings to his work a new perspective which is the direct result of two things: the time at which he was working (the periods of revolution in both France and America) and his claim that at least some of the work he produced was prophecy.

Blake was not alone in seeing these national revolutions as having eschatological significance. He and Richard Brothers – whom I have already mentioned in connection with Joanna Southcott – both believed themselves to be divinely inspired prophets who were to proclaim that biblical prophecy was being fulfilled in these struggles for freedom. The effect of this on Blake's work is to add a new dimension of dramatic intensity. He does not describe the signs and events of the end for their own sake, or portray them within the traditional biblical context. Instead they are used as a means of expressing his fervent convictions about these great revolutionary movements, and the drama is heightened still further by the inclusion of real people and places.

Revelation 17 and 18 present John's vision of the judgment and downfall of the great and sinful city of Babylon. The city is described allegorically: she is 'Babylon the great, mother of harlots and of earth's abominations' (Revelation 17:5). And John comments, 'I saw the woman drunk with the blood of the saints and the blood of the martyrs of Jesus' (v. 6). In Blake's poem 'America' the end of British rule in America is seen as the end of oppression by just such a figure. The arrival of the English forces is described in fearful apocalyptic terms:

> ...a terrible blast swept over the heaving sea.
> The eastern cloud rent: on his cliffs stood Albion's wrathful
>   Prince,
> A dragon form clashing his scales at midnight he arose,
> And flam'd red meteors round the land of Albion beneath;
> His voice, his locks, his awful shoulders, and his glowing eyes
> Appear to the Americans upon the cloudy night.
> (ll.14-18)

The plagues which are a characteristic of John's Babylon (Revelation 18:5) are directed against the Americans, only to rebound on their perpetrator:

> The red fires rag'd! the plagues recoil'd! then roll'd they back
>   with fury
> On Albion's Angels: then the Pestilence began in streaks of red
> Across the limbs of Albion's Guardian; the spotted plague
>   smote Bristol's,
> And the Leprosy London's Spirit, sickening all their bands.

> The millions sent up a howl of anguish and threw off their
>   hammer'd mail,
> And cast their swords & spears to earth, & stood, a naked
>   multitude.
> Albion's Guardian writhed in torment on the eastern sky,
> Pale quiv'ring toward the brain his blimmering eyes, teeth
>   chattering,
> Howling & shuddering, his legs quivering; convuls'd each
>   muscle & sinew.
> Sick'ning lay London's Guardian and the ancient miter'd York,
> Their heads on snowy hills, their ensigns sick'ning in the sky.
> (ll.177-87)

So the prophecy of Revelation is fulfilled:

> ...so shall her plagues come in a single day,
> pestilence and mourning and famine,
> and she shall be burned with fire;
> for mighty is the Lord God who judges her.
> (Revelation 18:8)

Blake's poem is an expansion of this theme, and the familiar language of prophecy and apocalyptic is dynamically revived as it describes the fury of war in which heavenly thrones and earthly kingdoms shudder at the fate of the colonizers. It is not just poetic licence. In this period of revolution, social and political upheavals are no longer just the starting point for apocalyptic writing and end-of-the-world speculation: in Blake's drama the two are inextricably interlinked. Indeed some social historians argue that it is only in this period that millennialism at last becomes rational and comprehensible.

The city and the end: two artists

One day in early May, while waiting for a connecting train, I visited the cathedral church of St Philip in the city of Birmingham. It is a small, not very beautiful eighteenth-century baroque building, which is somewhat overshadowed by civic buildings and the better-known landmark of St

151

Martins in the Bullring, whose blackened spire rises high above the shops and market area. On the edge of the cathedral's grounds there is a broken pillar, less than a metre high, which would normally be barely noticeable at the point where the grass meets the pavement. On that day, though, there were wreaths and bouquets of spring flowers piled up at its foot. It was so striking that a passing teenager stopped to ask, 'Has somebody died, then?' Seeing us looking and wondering, another passerby stopped too and provided the answer.

The broken pillar is a memorial to workers who were killed in the course of building the city's town hall. Every year, the Sunday before May Day is set aside to commemorate people killed in industrial accidents and looking again I could see that many of the wreaths laid there bore the names of leading trade unions. So the city honours its dead – keeping their memory alive in the heart of a city renowned as much for its character and vitality as for its slums and its unemployment. Inside the cathedral I found death too, although rather less painfully presented. Here it is obvious as soon as you get inside, as the building is dominated by the vicious red of some remarkable stained-glass windows designed by Edward Burne-Jones in 1897, a year before his own death.

At the east end above the altar, the ascending Christ, clad in red, is surrounded by angels as he takes his leave of his followers on the ground. To the left is the nativity window, where red angelic hosts surround the shepherds and the holy family. To the right there is a crucifixion scene, where the red recurs horrifically in the banners of Roman legions. The climax comes in the window at the opposite end of the cathedral, where Burne-Jones' Last Judgment fills the west window. Unlike the ascending Jesus, the Christ in judgment is garbed in white; he is surrounded by red angels, and in the foreground is the angel of the judgment, summoning with his trumpet the assembled darkened crowds below and creating an effective link between the judge and his people.

The expressions on the beautiful stylized faces that are just visible in the crowd reveal anxiety rather than outright fear. There is hope of salvation here, however uncomfortable the immediate present, and, as Burne-Jones' biographers tell us, destruction is played down: 'The crumbling world is very much a brown setting for the figures and there is almost a total absence of aggressive linear movement.' Just as the same artist turned the defeated King Arthur into a decorative symbol of a new and better age, so he seems to have sanitized the end of the world, in a way that clashes painfully with the reality of death displayed in the broken memorial outside. Burne-Jones has taken away the pain and idealized the men, women and children of the city as they wait to be gathered up into a new heaven, where Christ in glory, his crown of thorns and pierced hands clearly visible, is waiting for them.

Such a view of the end could only be transitory – a moment of calm in the *fin de siècle* turbulence. In the twentieth century, apocalypse is no longer the preserve of beautiful stained-glass windows. Already in the previous century artists had begun to depict contemporary events on a grand scale in a style which had hitherto been reserved for scenes from the Bible, literature or mythology. It was perhaps a natural extension of that to portray apocalypse now – in everyday familiar settings rather than on a predominantly supernatural level.

The years leading up to World War I seemed particularly suited to this type of artistic reaction. The four years between 1908 and 1912 saw the Messina earthquake and the sinking of the Titanic, together with an appearance of Halley's comet in 1910. All these events could be seen as portents, signs of human beings' lack of control and nature's revenge. The German Expressionist painter Ludwig Meidner (1884–1966) portrayed the end of the world in a series of paintings he later called 'apocalyptic landscapes'. His starting point was the desolation of the modern city, which is reflected in his pictures of Berlin. The German capital was then the fastest growing city in Europe: its population doubled between 1880 and 1910 and it was to double again by 1920. Meidner's pictures show houses collapsing into grotesque shapes, struck by pillars of fire from the sky and shaken by the moving earth beneath them. In the foreground he places human victims, who may be awaiting burial in this world or resurrection in the next.

Along with the other Expressionists of his generation, Meidner was influenced by Nietsche's *Thus Spake Zarathustra*, in which the purifying fire of the end is set within the city:

> Woe unto this great city! And I wish I already
> Saw the pillar of fire in which it will be burned.
> For such pillars of fire must precede the great noon.
> But this has its own time and its own destiny.

Perhaps as a result of Nietsche's work, Meidner's use of apocalyptic images is optimistic: a new, purer creation will emerge out of destruction, which then has to be seen as necessary and inevitable. So his work draws on ancient signs of the end of the world, especially the earthquakes, lightning and falling stars from Judaeo-Christian tradition, which testify to disorder in nature as well as among human beings, and sets them alongside the fire of Zoroastrianism; together these contribute to a secularized view of Christian resurrection, in the form of natural regeneration and renewal.

Meidner's work, although only a decade later than Burne-Jones' windows, is a lifetime away from the Pre-Raphaelites. In twentieth-century art and literature the language and imagery of biblical and post-biblical apocalyptic are assimilated into a secular context, repairing the post-medieval divide between sacred and secular. So Christian thought permeates even the most secular of works, such as Richard Strauss' *Alpensymphonie* (The 'Alpine' Symphony) which the composer called 'the Antichrist'. Its description in a letter that Strauss sent to Mahler suggests a humanistic rendering of millennial hope: 'It embodies moral purification through one's own strength, liberation through work, worship of eternal, glorious nature.' Conversely, the secular is a vital presence in many works of art with a religious theme. So the contemporary artist Roger Wagner depicts the crucifixion against the cooling towers of Didcot power station, which he sees as a metaphor for the chimneys of Auschwitz. Their belching black smoke filling the sky and the desolation of the mourners all tell of the portents and tribulation of the end, and buried deep within it the Christian hope of resurrection.

Tomorrow today

Our revels now are ended. These our actors,
As I foretold you, were all spirits, and
Are melted into air, into thin air;
And, like the baseless fabric of this vision,
The cloud-capp'd towers, the gorgeous palaces,
The solemn temples, the great globe itself,
Yea, all which it inherit, shall dissolve,
And, like this insubstantial pageant faded,
Leave not a rack behind. We are such stuff
As dreams are made on; and our little life
Is rounded with a sleep (*The Tempest*, Act 4, scene 1, 148-58).

So the weak and ageing Prospero begins to draw Shakespeare's play to a close. But is he simply reflecting on the outcome of events, pointing out that everything must come to an end, even the theatre (the Globe) in which the play takes place? Or is it that, as several critics have suggested, in his last plays Shakespeare is betraying the obsession of his time, the sense that, particularly after the death of Queen Elizabeth I, the old order had passed away, and, as Donne and Milton reiterated, theirs really were the latter days?

The multi-layered meaning of Shakespeare's play strikes me as one of the more subtle reflections of the things of the end in post-medieval literature. I can see nothing comparable in art today; the late twentieth century has moved beyond such ambiguities, despite the widespread interest in astrology and cults, and religious convictions about the end which seem to be as fervently expressed as ever.

This is not to say that the things of the end have disappeared from the face of modern literature. But already the nineteenth-century novelists were pigeonholing them, using them to portray such characters as the apocalyptic preachers in George Eliot's works, or the lower classes with their simple faith in the novels of Elizabeth Gaskell. So Mrs Gaskell's Bessy laments in *North and South* (1855), 'Sometimes I'm so tired out I think I cannot enjoy heaven without a piece of rest first. I'm rather afeared o' going straight there without getting a good sleep in the grave to set me up.' We all know the feeling, but the emphasis is surely on Bessy's lack of sophistication rather than a contribution to the premillennialist debate.

A notable contribution of modern literature has been to secularize the end-time. In his play *Huis clos (In Camera)* Jean-Paul Sartre memorably declared that hell is other people and demonstrated his thesis in his version of a truly eternal triangle: Inez (a homosexual) loves Estelle who loves Garcin (both heterosexuals) who loves Inez – and so on for ever. In March 1961 an exhibition opened at the Museum of Modern Art in Paris. Under the title of 'The Apocalypse' it brought together a selection of modern artists and writers whose subject was the book of Revelation. The exhibition was so popular that instead of running for a month, it was extended twice, running for twice as long as originally planned. One of the items was a specially written poem by Jean Cocteau, the poet, artist and film-director. Entitled 'Alors apparurent…' ('Then there appeared…'), it describes how people recognize that they are being judged; but they cannot read or write, and their language is meaningless. Like the characters in Sartre's play they suffer a dismal, but typically twentieth-century, fate: they are condemned to being permanently alienated – perpetual outsiders. In the hereafter they might think they would visit new worlds, but those worlds would want nothing to do with them.

In Julian Barnes' novel *A History of the World in 10½ Chapters* we cannot immediately be sure whether the final chapter, 'The Dream', is set in heaven or hell: 'I'd always had this dream... A dream of being judged... I wanted, oh, some kind of summing-up, I wanted my life looked at.' It turns out that heaven is what you want: 'We don't impose Heaven on people anymore... We listen to their needs. If they want it, they can have it; if not, not. And then of course they get the sort of Heaven they want.' Judgment too has been marginalized: 'People prefer to get what they want rather than what they deserve. Though some of them did get a little irritated that others weren't sufficiently maltreated. Part of their expectation of heaven seemed to be that other people would go to Hell.' Faced with enjoying what you want for ever is more of a nightmare than a dream, and the only solution is to go for a more conventional way of death.

Today's successors to the medieval drama of the end are more likely to be found in the realm of science fiction, especially in space travel. H.G. Wells' time traveller is echoed in the lone astronaut of *2001 – A Space Odyssey*, a 'last man' out beyond Jupiter. The destruction of the wicked city of Babylon is repeated in the devastation of American cities as the world fights for survival in *Independence Day*. For the post-modernist writer or artist the end of the world is essentially an individual experience, even though the old imagery seems to be too deeply engrained to be left wholly out of account. At the same time there has also been a gradual shift in interpretation of the end in religous thought. What was once universally acknowledged has tended to become the province of specialist groups – specific sects or denominations, even political parties. And it is these variations in interpreting the things of the end that are the subject of the next chapter.

References

Julian Barnes, *A History of the World in 10½ Chapters*, Jonathan Cape, 1989.

William Blake, *Poems and Prophecies*, edited by Max Plowman, Everyman's Library, Dent, London, 1927.

Geoffrey Chaucer, *The Canterbury Tales*, translated by David Wright, Oxford University Press, 1985.

Carol S. Eliel, *The Apocalyptic Landscapes of Ludwig Meidner*, Prestel, 1989.

Clarke Garrett, *Respectable Folly: Millenarians and the French Revolution in France and England*, Johns Hopkins University Press, Baltimore and London, 1975.

Elizabeth Gaskell, *North and South*, 1855; Penguin Books, 1994.

Steven Goldsmith, *Unbuilding Jerusalem: Apocalypse and Romantic Representation*, Cornell University Press, 1993.

Martin Harrison and Bill Waters, *Burne-Jones*, Barrie and Jenkins, London, 1973.

W.W. Heist, *The Fifteen Signs before Doomsday*, Michigan State College Press, 1952.

E. Le Roy (editor), *Le Jour du Jugement*, Paris, 1902.

R. Mantou (editor), *Les 15 Signes du Jugement Dernier*, 1965.

Cynthia Marshall, *Last Things and Last Plays: Shakespearean Eschatology*, Southern Illinois University Press, 1991.

Jean-Paul Sartre, *Huis clos (In Camera)*, Paris, Gallimard, 1947.

Mary Shelley, *The Last Man*, 1825; World Classics, Oxford University Press, 1994.

John Stokes (editor), *Fin de Siècle, Fin du Globe: Fears and Fantasies of the Late Nineteenth Century*, Macmillan, 1992.

F. Whitehead (editor), *La Chanson de Roland (The Song of Roland)*, Blackwell, 1942.

Chapter 9

Interpreting the End

Clov: 'Do you believe in the life to come?'
Hamm: 'Mine was always that.'

Samuel Beckett, *Endgame*

The events of the end, prophesied since historical records began, along with the signs that precede them and elaborate attempts to date them, are all part of our cultural heritage. But although the whole panoply of ideas and symbols is developed most carefully within major religious systems, no one religion can completely contain them. Seemingly, for as long as the concept of an end-time has been around, it has been appropriated by people with agendas of their own. Indeed, these things are there to be appropriated almost by definition, because signs and events do not in themselves constitute explanations of the end. So for some who seek to explain, the agenda is a religious one, while for others it is a political one. For others still, like the characters in a Beckett play, there is little rhyme or reason to what they are trying to say, but the traditional images of the end are nonetheless there to help them say it.

Christianity has seen many attempts to interpret its teaching on the end in the light of contemporary experiences or obsessions. Most of these have one thing in common: they insist on interpreting as literal truth at least some biblical writings which do not easily bear such an interpretation.

Such an attitude is not, of course, confined to people whose particular concern is with the end of time. Christian fundamentalists in general, according to Professor James Barr, are distinctive for their emphasis on the inerrancy of the Bible, their hostility to modern theology and academic critical methods applied to the Bible, and their conviction that those who do not share their beliefs are not 'true' Christians. What is unfortunately often the case is that fundamentalists, convinced that scripture is infallible, tend to hold a similar conviction that their own interpretation of biblical writing is equally infallible. My own view has long been that it is perfectly possible to believe that biblical writing is inspired by God, without having to insist either that figurative language has to be understood literally, or that what God says to people on one occasion has necessarily to be put in identical terms many centuries later.

Within Christianity, one of the most lasting outworkings of the 'literal truth' approach to the Bible, and also one of the most creative, has been the doctrine of the dispensationalists, who came into being in the middle of the nineteenth century and are still making their presence felt at the end of the twentieth.

'Jesus is Coming'

When this world begins to rock
Infidels and sceptics mock
There's a time of awful anguish coming on.
Oh what groans and bitter pains
When the Antichrist shall reign,
When the tribulation enters I'll be gone.

Dispensationalism has its roots in the Brethren movement (sometimes called the Plymouth Brethren) in England and Ireland which began around 1830. Like other Christian groups at various times it was formed out of widespread dissatisfaction with the worldliness of the established church and was characterized by the rejection of an ordained ministry and an insistence on the hope that Christ's return was imminent. The Brethren remained a minority sect but the dispensationalist movement which emerged from it – as the result of a quarrel between two of their leaders – proved to be far more influential. The spread of dispensationalist teaching owed much to two publications: a book by W.E. Blackstone, published in 1878, called *Jesus is Coming*, and the better known Scofield Bible (published by Oxford University Press in 1909), which added extensive notes and comments to the text of the King James Bible according to the dispensationalist manner of interpretation.

At the heart of dispensationalism, and a good illustration of its approach to scripture, are verses from 1 Thessalonians:

> The dead in Christ will rise first; then we who are alive, who are left, shall be caught up together with them in the clouds to meet the Lord in the air; and so we shall always be with the Lord (1 Thessalonians 4:16-17).

In context these verses form part of the answer to a question which clearly bothered the early Christians: what will happen to those who are already dead when Jesus returns. The writer reassures his readers that, when the time comes, those who have died in the faith will be raised to life, as Paul wrote to the Corinthians: 'The trumpet will sound, and the dead will be raised imperishable and we shall be changed' (1 Corinthians 15:52). The problem in 1 Thessalonians is the writer's vision of what will happen to the living. The dispensationalists argue that the phrase 'in the air', far from being a first-century writer's attempt to describe the indescribable, must mean exactly what it says. When Christ returns the living faithful will rise into the air to meet him, an event which they call the rapture. And around this is constructed a whole new system of interpreting time and its end.

According to dispensationalists, the resurrection of the dead and the rapture of the living are to take place before the millennium, that is before Christ's return and before the rise of Antichrist and the tribulation that is to precede the end. The picture is complicated by the literal interpretation of other parts of scripture, most notably Old Testament prophecies concerning the future of Israel, which dispensationalists say must mean the earthly Israel (unlike early Christian theologians who reinterpreted them to refer to the community of the church). Therefore, if the end is near, so too must be the Jews' return to their homeland, as prophesied, for instance, in Ezekiel 36 and 37.

When that expectation is added in, the system works like this. At the time of the rapture those Christians who are deemed worthy are caught up into the air to be with the Lord, who comes down to meet the true church, his bride. Then follows a short period of tribulation (literally the three and a half years or 1,260 days), after which Jesus appears again with his saints to judge the living. After that comes the 1,000-year rule of Christ, followed by the unloosing of Satan before the final judgment and eternity. It is a system which creates two separate classes of Christians, three comings of Christ instead of two, and a number of separate times of judgment.

What makes this more than just another theory of the order of events of the end is the view of the church that it contains. Briefly, the period of the church, from Pentecost to the rapture, is seen as a hiatus or parenthesis: an interruption in God's dealings with his chosen people Israel, which can be resumed once the church (or at least the more godly members of it) is taken up. The final verses of Daniel 9 are cited in support of this: the first sixty-nine of the seventy weeks of years which are to put an end to Israel's sin (9:24) are taken to be a time which ends with Jesus' triumphal entry into Jerusalem – the Jews' final opportunity to acknowledge him as their Messiah. Then comes the period of the church – the week in which God makes 'a strong covenant with many' (9:27), and in the first part of which 'sacrifice and offering... cease'. In this view, which regularly emphasizes Old Testament teaching at the expense of the New, the Christian age is no more than a hiccup, a parenthesis in the ways of God.

The term 'dispensation' reflects a view of time which, paradoxically, owes more to metaphor and allegory than to literal meaning of scripture. It is defined as a period of time during which people's obedience to God is tested in the face of some particular revelation of his will. The whole of time is divided into seven dispensations of unequal length. In Blackstone's version these are innocence (Eden), antediluvian (a period of freedom in which conscience is the only restraint), post-diluvian (the age of government, culminating in the destruction of Sodom), patriarchal, Mosaic (up to the crucifixion), Christian (from Pentecost to judgment) and the millennium (the final judgment). Two of these ages are said to contain examples, or types, of the forthcoming rapture: there is Enoch, taken up in the second dispensation, and Elijah in the Mosaic age. Unwilling, perhaps, to let his scheme tail off with eternity, Blackstone suggests that the coming of a new heaven and a new earth may mark the beginning of a fresh series of ages or dispensations.

There are, of course, many issues raised by dispensationalist teaching, not least, for orthodox Christians, the marginalization of Christ's crucifixion. But, as we shall see, one has proved to be of enduring concern for the end of time: the insistence that the Jews should be restored to Israel so that God's work with them can be resumed. Indeed, under this scheme, the people left to enjoy Christ's 1,000-year reign of peace will be essentially Jewish. Blackstone thought the end was near because in 1907 he saw Jews beginning to return to Israel, spurred on by 'anti-Semitic agitations' in a number of European countries and by the construction of a railway system within Israel itself. Other signs of 'Christ's speedy coming' which he notes include apostasy (particularly the church's failure to preach on the approaching end), spiritualism (he lumps together Christian Scientists and Buddhists), the mail (which facilitates the distribution of obscene literature), worldwide evangelism (thanks to the effectiveness of Victorian missionary societies), and political dangers. He wrote: 'All Europe is practically a soldier's camp, with 23,000,000 of drilled men ready to fly at each other in a universal war, with weapons so ingenious and deadly as to put all the past record beneath the shadow of comparison.'

Dispensationalism has been criticized for being dependent on 'a faulty and unscriptural literalism', although, as I have hinted, this literalism is sometimes turned to highly creative ends. Barr comments: 'As a feat of the imagination it might well compare with the apocalyptic poems of Blake, and indeed the latter may have done something to influence its origin.' Yet the concept of the rapture of Christians continues to have a great following, particularly in the United States, where apparently one can buy rapture watches (with slogans such as 'one hour nearer the end') and car bumper stickers ('When the rapture comes, this car will be driverless'). There are rapture comics. I have seen one which tells the story in comic strips of a hospital at the rapture. Doctors and nurses scurry along the corridors in bewilderment and panic: all the babies – the human innocents – have vanished from their cots.

By any standards this scenario is pretty far-fetched, although there is a certain irony in the fact that it originates with people whose view of scripture professes to rule out any kind of novelty or adaptation to present-day circumstances. But it is all fairly harmless, at least in comparison with the policy towards the Jewish people which today is being vigorously pursued by dispensationalists and other like-minded pre-millennialists.

Restoring Israel

The Jews have always had an unenviable role in Christian eschatology. We have seen how in the Middle Ages this took the form of depicting Antichrist as a Jew, while the idea that the Jews must be converted and restored to Israel before the end has led to some very dubious Christian attitudes towards them. Since some Christians believe that this conversion and restoration must take place before they themselves have any hope of glory, their motive in promoting missionary activities among the Jews or in politically encouraging their return can easily be seen as self-interest. At the end of World War II the revelation of the horrors of the Holocaust added Christian guilt to the impulse to return Jews to their homeland, although an opposite view was that the fate of the Jews was prophetic – a sign of their suffering in the tribulation at the end. In the highly complex field of Middle East politics, many American premillennialists, including leading politicians and the evangelist Billy Graham, have supported Israel almost unquestioningly.

In the North Yorkshire city of Hull there is a company called Good News Travels. According to press reports, in the five years since the break up of the Soviet Union this company was responsible for transporting 20,000 Jews from all over the Ukraine to Kiev airport, where they could board flights to Israel, in a project cringingly named 'Exobus'. The organizers justify their actions by referring to the Old Testament prophets, Jeremiah, Isaiah and Ezekiel: 'We are living in the end-times and… God is gathering his people from the land of the north to Israel and… Christian gentiles must help them. Prophecies 2,500 years old are being fulfilled in the 1990s.'

The Jews who take advantage of this bus journey seem, by all accounts, to be bemused by it all. Some are clearly glad to be on their way, although the organizers' promotion of Israel as an idyllic haven with no reference to its precarious political situation seems to be somewhat economical with the truth. For the state of Israel, each new wave of Jewish immigrants adds to the burden on its social services. But the volunteers staffing the Exobus seem not to want to know. One is quoted as saying: 'When I get a Jew to the airport, I feel I have saved them. This work is as important as bringing people to Christ.' Is this Christian concern in action, or simply enlightened self-interest?

However, it is not in Britain but in the United States that Christian evangelical support of Israel has been strongest, and this goes back to well before the rise of political Zionism. It is probably due in large part to the fact that dispensationalism has always had a greater following in the States than in its country of origin.

In 1916, the dispensationalist Blackstone organized what he called a 'memorial' to the United States President, Woodrow Wilson. It was a petition asking him to convene an international conference which would call for Palestine to be handed to the Jews, a move which won widespread support among the major Protestant churches. It was also endorsed by leaders of the Zionist movement, who were apparently aware of the nature of Blackstone's teaching but were nonetheless prepared to work with him.

However, a recent Jewish commentator has suggested that the Zionists may not have known the full extent of Blackstone's involvement in Christian missionary work among the Jews, which went back to the founding of the Chicago Hebrew Mission in 1887. There was also Blackstone's argument that only Orthodox and Zionist Jews would return to Israel. Reform (or liberal) Jews would be doomed to perish at the tribulation, along with non-Protestant Christians.

In the event, although Wilson was sympathetic he did not accept the petition publicly, perhaps because he feared the repercussions of removing Palestine from what was then the Turkish empire. And after the 1919 peace conference which favoured the idea of an Arab state in 'Greater Syria', Blackstone's moves were soon forgotten, along with his vision of America as a 'modern Cyrus' who would help restore the Jews to Israel. It was only really in the 1970s that the United States invested considerable political power in working on Israel's behalf. Yaakov Ariel ends his study of the 1916 petition with an ironic reflection:

> Today's fundamentalists… do not see the Jewish state in terms of the security and safety of the Jews. Rather, the establishment of Israel is perceived as merely one step towards the millennial kingdom. The existence of the new state is no more than a temporary stage in the advancement of the eschatological timetable, a vehicle predestined to prepare the ground for the messianic age.

Hal Lindsey and the Rapture

It is claimed that the best-selling non-fiction book of the 1970s was Hal Lindsey's *The Late Great Planet Earth*, which went on to sell 32 million copies worldwide. Lindsey's premise then and since has been that the end of the world is 'breathtakingly close', as he put it in a 1996 television interview. His published writings present an intriguing mixture of scriptural prophecy and pure speculation, which is typically presented as solid fact.

Lindsey has done much to popularize dispensationalist-style pre-millennialism. Like Blackstone and his followers he sees the restoration of Israel as central to what he calls 'the end-time scenario', an idea which had already gained a new impetus with the foundation of the state of Israel after World War II. Unlike Blackstone, though, he gives increasing weight to the book of Revelation and less to the Old Testament prophets, and he devotes much more space to identifying contemporary world events which seem to fit the symbolic details of Revelation – the ecumenical movement, a growing drug culture, hostility between East and West. For years Lindsey has maintained that the world is on the verge of 'the final fateful period immediately preceding the Second Coming of Christ' – namely, seven years of tribulation, although the unimagined break-up of the Soviet Union appears to have taken the sting out of many of Lindsey's prophecies.

In a 1983 book called *The Rapture: Truth or Consequences*, Lindsey draws parallels between events he predicts and the opening of the seven seals in Revelation. For example, the opening of the third seal heralds global economic catastrophe:

> After war breaks out in the Middle East, oil from the Persian Gulf will be halted and worldwide economic chaos will set in. Food will become scarce and very expensive (Revelation 6:5-6).

When the fifth seal is opened Antichrist gains absolute control of people through economics: every person in the world has an identity number with the prefix 666, without which they can do nothing – a development made possible by computers and a cashless society. And so it goes on. Speaking more recently Lindsey has claimed that the end is being hastened by the rise of Europe as a world power which, for example, has had the temerity to try to intervene in Bosnia in place of the United States. This, he says, is the beginning of a 'revived Roman empire'.

Lindsey also develops the idea of rapture (which he wants to call 'the great snatch') beyond that envisaged by the early dispensationalists. In particular he sees the writer of Revelation as being 'raptured':

> John was hurtled by God's Spirit through time up to the end of the twentieth century, shown the actual cataclysmic events of the Tribulation, then returned to the first century and told to write about what he had witnessed.

Revelation 8 was thus for John a 'thermonuclear naval battle in terms of his first-century experience'. Revelation has become the 'only book in the Bible specifically written to detail the events of the tribulation' – although sceptics might see in this the insidious influence of science fiction.

Lindsey's writings and the style of worship they have provoked are a curious mixture of self-satisfied triumphalism and gloom. Because of his desire to fit every contemporary development into his end-time system, no innovation can be seen as good in itself. Computer technology and European unity are only to be welcomed insofar as they hasten the end, in much the same way as Blackstone viewed socialism and the postal services; otherwise they merely facilitate the spread of the power of Antichrist. But none of this matters to the true believer. As the chorus to the song quoted earlier puts it:

> I'll be gone, I'll be gone,
> Oh when the tribulation enters I'll be gone!
> Soon the trumpet loud shall sound
> With a shout I'll leave the ground,
> When the tribulation enters I'll be gone!

'The Trumpeter'

Although the extravagances I have described are typically associated with extreme Protestant groups, they are by no means confined to them. Quite by chance I came across a publication by a Roman Catholic, possibly a member of a fringe religious order, who called himself 'The Trumpeter'. His *Parables and Predictions* published in 1987 are said to have been written under the guidance of 'one or more of the many Blessed Souls who are members of God's eternal Kingdom'.

The second half of the book contains seventy-five predictions which begin at the end of the 1980s. Many of them are so precise that their non-fulfilment is evident, but they still make rather grim reading. All kinds of elements are mixed in, from biblical apocalyptic signs to environmental concerns and personal hobbyhorses. The first few predictions focus on political developments and events in the church; there are to be revolutions in France and Italy, the latter deliberately incited by Communists to divert attention from their plans to assassinate Pope John Paul II, who is eventually spirited away by St Michael to a place of safety. The pope then seems to take on the role of the medieval Angelic Pope. During a worldwide 'Great Cold' which lasts for seven weeks, John Paul 'bilocates' all over the world teaching and preaching, only to be killed at the hands of 'Anti-Pope'. Again this seems to owe more than a little to science fiction.

Between the oddities (all test-tube babies will be agents of the devil), there is a great deal of ill-disguised traditional eschatology: Enoch and Elijah return and are killed; there are plagues, earthquakes, national uprisings, and darkness and floods over the earth thanks to a comet striking the Caribbean. When the millennium comes the children and adults who have been taken up in the rapture (which is not described) return to earth, and resurrection and judgment follow on with little to distinguish them from orthodox Christian belief.

My reason for dwelling on this particular publication is partly to demonstrate how pervasive the old ideas of the end continue to be, and how easily they can be combined with modern developments and indeed with modern apprehensions, such as the fear of environmental or cosmological disaster. What it also shows, though, is how a different kind of Christian theology can equally well be intertwined with the events of the end. The Trumpeter accepts biblical prophecy without fussing unduly about its literal truth. He is much more concerned with portraying the evil forces as those that are opposed to the Roman Catholic status quo (the Anti-Pope imposes a 'One World Church' and abolishes the use of the word 'catholic'), and with showing the righteous as people who observe certain Catholic practices, such as praying the Rosary. The Trumpeter's own preference seems to be for religious communities, since life in the millennium appears rich in vocations to the religious life, while the only people permitted to teach faith and doctrine will be the priests.

Oppression and the end

The dispensationalist system was constructed on the basis of a number of carefully selected biblical passages. Believers then typically interpret current events or concerns in the light of these and other texts which seem to fit the system. So Hal Lindsey is concerned to 'harmonize' biblical texts so that they fit his scheme, hence the idea of the writer of Revelation experiencing the events of the end two millennia ahead of time. However, dispensationalists and others often opt for a narrower focus, taking isolated texts as a basis for their own prophetic interpretations. Billy Graham did this when he took the four horses of Revelation 6 as restating four signs of the end from Matthew 24: false religion, war and peace, famine and plague, and death and suffering. It becomes a dramatic metaphor, as Graham encourages his readers to 'put our ears to the ground and hear their hoofbeats growing louder by the day'. He also lays claim to a prophetic vision:

> With John I have heard the distant sound of hoofbeats. I have seen the evil riders on the horizons of our lives... there is serious trouble ahead for our world, for all of us who live in it, and in the four horsemen of the Apocalypse there is both a warning and wisdom for those troubled days ahead.

Yet I find there is something fundamentally unsatisfying about these publications. Typically it is not the end of time, but a single facet or image of it, which becomes the subject of intense scrutiny. Not only does this lead to some bizarre interpretations, but the wider context risks becoming blurred, or dropping out of sight altogether. To concentrate on the evils of modern communications or on returning Jews to Israel is to risk losing touch with the huge sweep of the biblical narrative from creation in Genesis to the new creation of John's great vision, and all that has happened along the way.

In order for the events of the end to make any kind of sense, either intellectually or emotionally, they need to be set in a context, traditionally a theological one. But what happens when that theological context is perceived to be inadequate? In the last couple of hundred years two distinct answers have emerged: either you replace theology with a different system or you find a new theology. And in each case this has happened in response to situations characterized above all by oppression.

A new theology

One of the most striking new theologies to emerge in the twentieth century, which gives a proper place to the things of the end, is liberation theology. As is well known, this has come to be particularly associated with theologians in South America who live and work among some of the world's poorest and most marginalized people. Liberation theology is a commitment to 'suffering with' the poor, who are not to be the object of charity, but subjects and agents of their own liberation. As a study by Boff and Boff puts it:

> Underlying liberation theology is a prophetic and comradely commitment to the life, cause and struggle of those millions of

debased and marginalized human beings, a commitment to ending this historical-social iniquity.

This commitment relates to the things of the end in a significant way: it is only when God's children have been given back their freedom and their dignity that the idea of the Kingdom of God, a utopia of freedom, justice, love and peace, whether in this world or the next, can have any credibility at all.

Liberation theology is prophetic in that it denounces oppression and utopian in that it has a dream of a society of freed men and women. For Christians that dream has already been realized in anticipation by Jesus in his death and resurrection. But how is it to be made a reality for the oppressed? Once again Matthew 25 is a key text. If believers accept the words of Christ at the time of judgment – 'as you did it to the least of these my brethren, you did it to me' (v. 40) – then one of the main motivations in bringing about liberation has to be an eschatological one: the idea that at the end of time we will be judged according to how we have treated the poor:

At the supreme moment of history, when our eternal salvation or damnation will be decided, what will count will be our attitude of acceptance or rejection of the poor... Only those who commune in his history with the poor and needy, who are Christ's sacraments, will commune definitively with Christ.

In terms of this theology, the new Jerusalem of Revelation 21 will only come into being when the old earth with all its oppressions has passed away:

The new earth will be a gift of God and the fruit of human effort. What was begun in history will continue in eternity: the kingdom of the freed, living as brothers and sisters in the great house of the Father.

The events of the end are again to some extent placed under human control. The primary task is to work for a society free from exploitation, to translate the eschatological hope of God's kingdom into the hope of personal and social freedom in the here and now. Only then does the next step become possible, which is communion with God in a totally redeemed creation.

A new society

One summer in the mid-1980s I flew to Auckland and drove the length of New Zealand's North Island, and on down through most of the South Island as well. Probably my most abiding impression is the brilliance of the night sky, in the absence of the light pollution that is a fact of life in European towns and cities. But the Southern sky was run a close second by Maori culture, which, at least in North Island, is inescapable and not a little disturbing. One of its most distinctive features, seen on monuments and carved posts which mark boundaries or commemorate the dead, are carvings of the god Tu, who characteristically has his tongue sticking out. Even so, it was not so much Tu as the influence of Christianity which sparked off a millennial cult in the nineteenth century and led to a bitter war between the Maoris and the British colonizers. It also highlighted an interpretation of the end of the world rather different from anything I have described hitherto.

Besides imposing imperial rule on their colonies, the British brought their religion with them and soon set about converting the indigenous peoples. Indeed it is likely that the Maori revolt in the 1860s was directed as much against Christian missionaries as against the military, but by then Christianity had already permeated their religious thinking. So it was that in 1862 a Maori called Te Ua claimed to have had a vision of the angel Gabriel, who revealed a new religion in place of the 'false' English one. The religion was called Pai-Marire ('good and merciful') and, taking up the belief that the Maoris were descended from the tribes of Judah, Te Ua cast himself in the role of a new Moses.

Te Ua and his followers called themselves the Hau-hau (as a verb 'hau' means to attack, and as an exclamation it means breath or life), and they saw it as their sacred duty to wipe out the white colonists, believing that legions of angels would help them drive the English back into the sea. In the Hau-hau movement, and others like it, religion and politics are virtually indistinguishable, since salvation is equated with reclaiming land and power for the indigenous people. Such movements are by their very nature militaristic and the result for the Maoris was years of bloodshed.

In this context the end of the world takes on a very specific meaning – victory over the oppressor. The Hau-haus believed that driving the English out of New Zealand would bring the present time to an end and usher in the millennium. Christian tradition is translated into terms acceptable to the natives, and in this case it was believed that once the English had gone the Maori dead would rise again in an atmosphere of millennial peace, with Te Ua appearing as either Moses or Christ. Interestingly, the Jews were to be gathered into New Zealand where they would form a single people with the Maoris in a new life. The Italian anthropologist Vittorio Lanternari believes that this sprang from the teaching of Christian missionaries – but whereas the missionaries taught the history of Israel as a model of religious strength, the Maoris saw in it a model of political action. Of course the Hau-haus were doomed to fail in the face of overwhelming colonial opposition. In 1886 Te Ua himself surrendered to the English and was treated leniently, but the fight had already ended some years before.

The intermingling of Judaeo-Christian ideas with basic elements from native religions crops up in various parts of the world, and is closely allied to a belief that the world will end, or at least come to a final state of perfection, once the foreign oppressor is driven out. These religious-political movements, which affected American Indians and Polynesians in the nineteenth century and continued among Africans and Melanesians in the twentieth, do not see the end of time as something to be feared. With such movements, as Professor Burridge says, the millennium has moved beyond purely Judaeo-Christian connotations: it is 'equivalent to salvation and to redemption itself'. He goes on to argue that these movements and their prophets are necessary as a focus for action, to bring order to unordered activities. Seen like that, he concludes, 'as an experiment in finding new ways, a millenarian movement never fails entirely.'

Star gazing

In 1524 much of western Europe was in a state of panic. A German astrologer, one Johann Stoeffler, based in Tübingen – a town better known nowadays for its theology faculty than for its astrology – had predicted that the world would end in a flood, which would begin on 20 February. Stoeffler's claim was based on a rare astronomical phenomenon – the conjunction of all the planets in the sign of Pisces, the fish, hence the water. Such was the power of the printed almanacs which publicized the prophecy that even national leaders took fright. The Elector of Brandenburg fled to the mountains, taking with him his family and his astrologer for good measure; Charles V of Spain and many of his subjects made for higher ground; while in France the President of the University of Toulouse, perhaps seeing himself as a latter-day Noah, built a boat.

The fact that 20 February 1534 was completely dry in no way affected the credibility of astrologers in the eyes of their followers (and in any case a month of rain soon followed). It takes more than a missing flood to discredit a science which was refined by the Ancient Babylonians more than five centuries before Christ. Whereas the followers of the great religions trust in their faith to make at least some sense of the universe, astrologers have always used the stars to the same end. It is likely that the 'wise' men who visited the infant Jesus were astrologers, who clearly enjoyed prestige and influence among the ruling class.

Astrology is the belief that the movements of heavenly bodies can be interpreted so as to provide information about life on earth. Although at its most sophisticated it is based on complex observations far removed from the horoscopes that figure in today's popular press, there has always been a question mark as to how objective the interpretations of the data might be. When a society goes through such a period of upheaval that people begin to speculate about the end, it is more than likely that astrologers' predictions also adopt a doomsday slant. As Defoe puts it in the *Journal of the Plague Year*, 'One Mischief always introduces another.' He depicts people's fear of the plague as being whipped up by astrologers who 'added some of the Conjunctions of the Planets in a malignant Manner... one of which Conjunctions was to happen, and did happen, in October... and they filled the Peoples Heads with Predictions or these Signs of the Heavens, intimating, that these Conjunctions foretold Drought, Famine, and Pestilence.' As fear increased, so the 'Fortune-tellers, Cunning-men and Astrologers' multiplied in the capital.

Astrology is not of course just concerned with major events like these. In the sixteenth century astrology was important for deciding on the proper time for surgery – and perhaps this is understandable, given the state of the art. And there was a widespread belief that it was dangerous to take any medicine at the height of summer, during the so-called 'dog days'. In the sixteenth century, too, astrology was still regarded as a science. Perhaps for this reason it was not forbidden by the church, despite the fact that people often associated it with magic and witchcraft.

The best-known astrologer of them all, Nostradamus, learned astrology from his maternal grandfather. An outbreak of plague in Southern France in the 1540s was responsible for his rise to fame as an astrologer – for he followed the trend in attributing the plague to astrological causes. Astrology was also much in fashion at the French court, where Nostradamus' predictions were taken extremely seriously, especially when his prophecy of the death of Charles IX was fulfilled. As we have already seen, his prophecies of future disasters were vague and general, and open to all kinds of interpretations. But while many people have related them to events that have already taken place, the prophecies have never proved to be a satisfactory base for predicting the future. Yet such was Nostradamus' power that after he died in 1566, the belief grew up that he had buried himself alive, and anyone approaching him would die – a bizarre perversion of the myth of the vanished hero who would return in his people's hour of need.

Astrology does, however, figure in the interpretation of the time of the end in the myth of the 'Great Year'. This is the belief that society moves through periods of history which constitute 'years' which, like calendar years, can be said to have their own seasons. So astrologers have looked at significant points in human history, such as the age of the classical Hebrew prophets or the Ancient Greeks, and have tried to show that they were accompanied by major astronomical phenomena. The myth includes the idea that disasters precede a golden age, and that the change from one age to another may be brought about by a heroic or divine figure. Since the French Revolution, political revolutionary movements have been added as possible cataclysmic events.

Such ideas obviously have something in common with Christian belief in Christ's rule for 1,000 years, as well as with other religious or secular systems which expect a return to a lost Golden Age. But the similarity ends there. Both Jews and Christians understand time to be linear, coming to an end at a certain point, while systems like the Great Year tend towards a cyclical view of time. The Golden Age is reached, only to begin to decline, and the whole process begins all over again.

Even so, it is unlikely that the average reader of horoscopes, who believes that there is 'something in it all', is thinking on such a grandiose scale. Many such readers, lacking any firm religious faith, seem happy to believe anything the astrologers tell them and they are a gullible and receptive audience for every new interpretation of Nostradamus' ramblings. As David Sexton, a book reviewer for a national newspaper, faced with such publications as *Nostradamus' Prophecies for Women* and *The Elixirs of Nostradamus*, and exasperated at the 'shameful lot of stuff and nonsense' put out by reputable publishing houses, exclaimed in horror, 'Can the *Nostradamus Work-Out Book* be far behind?'

Fearing the end

When I was a student of linguistics in the late 1960s, the biggest name in the field was Professor Noam Chomsky from the Massachusetts Institute of Technology, who had formulated an exciting new theory of language a few years before. When he came to Oxford to lecture we were captivated by his comparative youth and by his ability to talk on mathematics, philosophy and language with equal facility. Not long after that he turned to politics and became a formidable campaigner against the Vietnam War. So perhaps it was inevitable that in 1996 he should pop up in yet another context – reflecting soberly on US society and its obsession with cults and with the end of the world. His judgment on America was brief and to the point: 'This is the most frightened country I've ever seen.'

One way in which such fear is manifested is when people identify contemporary institutions – which may make them fearful for one reason or another – with events of the end. The possibility of the United States collaborating with the United Nations to produce a 'globalist government' is an example cited by Professor Chomsky. If this perceived movement towards worldwide domination is viewed as facilitating the rise of Antichrist, then it becomes a sign that the end is near. For believers at least, the fear is thus rationalized and contained; they may even welcome such developments since it brings the longed-for end nearer.

Another way in which people's fear may find expression is in the formation of cults. The most extreme Doomsday cults are those that watch for signs of the end in order that their members might destroy themselves first, since the alternative is too dreadful to remain alive for. Now there is little doubt that the late twentieth century has seen the proliferation of cults of all kinds. In 1994 Inform, a London organization set up to research religious movements, had 2,000 cults on its books. A year later it was claimed that in France alone there were some 1,300 cults with followings of more than 150,000 people.

It may be that cults have always been with us in substantial numbers and have only become more widely known thanks to modern communications. Some cults have retained many characteristics of one of the major religions from which they spring; others may have their roots in ancient pagan cults. Back in the Roman empire it is well known that a wide range of religious beliefs were tolerated, with the sole proviso that the Emperor was worshipped as well, and for a while Christianity was treated as just another cult, but with its members being persecuted for their refusal to worship the emperor-gods. Early evidence of a cult of the sun, encouraged by the third-century Roman emperors, is revealed in Britain by ancient burial sites: the bodies were laid out with the feet pointing east, so that they could rise up and face the rising sun on the day of resurrection.

Some cults arise in response to specific social circumstances, and are not necessarily related to fears of the end. In the late nineteenth century, a religious crisis in the form of conflict between those who clung to traditional beliefs and those who favoured an atheism based on the supremacy of science, led to a variety of responses, including alternative forms of spiritual expression. The work of a number of artists of the 1890s who formed a group calling themselves the Nabis (from the Hebrew word for 'prophet') reflects their attempt to bring together Christian themes and the teachings of other religions. Elie Ranson's painting 'Christ and Buddha' of 1890 includes a Buddha figure, a Hindu lotus and an Arabic inscription. Behind their public art the group evolved its own secret ceremonies, met together in a 'temple' and called one another 'Brother'.

Many, if not most, cults seem to have discernible elements from Christianity or other world religions which have either been intermingled or developed in some other way. But they are not necessarily always what they seem. In October 1994, a cult called the Order of the Solar Temple hit the headlines when forty-eight of its members were found dead in Switzerland and five more in Canada. Fourteen months later, sixteen more cult members died in the Vercors region of France. The cult itself seemed to be a mixture of Christian and occult beliefs – its members wore white copes decorated with a red cross – although only an elite inner circle knew what the doctrines actually were. In Canada the community had its own nuclear shelter, while in Switzerland it was suggested that they were stockpiling weapons in readiness for the end of the world, although there has been no reason to link them with other Doomsday sects or with eschatological beliefs. What is in a way more sinister is that the whole set-up could have been a financial scam. Members of the Order all paid fees and some of them were extremely wealthy. Whether or not the sect's founder was among those killed in the various massacres remains an open question.

Interpretations of the end are as varied as the social and cultural circumstances that produce them and the approach of the year 2,000 will have spawned a number of new millennial movements and interpretations. But along with this go movements whose origins are related not so much to the date as to developments in alternative spiritualities, space technology, and the ever-present interest in unidentified flying objects and a belief in beings from outer space. Traditional lines of apocalyptic thought are often still in evidence in these cases: 'The Bible is a UFO compendium,' declared the Executive Secretary of the Aetherius Society – a London-based 'ufology' centre. For him the biblical sorting of the wheat from the chaff (Matthew 3:12) will happen when another master steps out among humankind from a UFO.

Not surprisingly, people who seem to be particularly gullible in their beliefs about the end are liable to be taken advantage of. In September 1992 a Korean pastor was preaching that the rapture would take place the following month, when he was arrested for having accepted £2 million from his followers and converting some of it illegally into US dollars. He was then found to have purchased more than £200,000 of bonds which were due to mature in 1995. This would have been three years into the time of tribulation, when, he claimed, money would be worthless.

What is perhaps most remarkable about the situation at the end of the twentieth century is the persistence of the traditional symbolism associated with the end. And despite all the technological advances, the belief that scriptural texts still somehow include a pointer to the end, albeit in encoded form, is a very resilient one. Will any of this change in the twenty-first century?

References

Oswald T. Allis, *Prophecy and the Church: An Examination of the Claim of Dispensationalists that the Christian Church is a Mystery Parenthesis which Interrupts the Fulfilment to Israel of the Kingdom Prophecies of the Old Testament*, London, James Clarke & Co. Ltd, 1945.

Yaakov Amiel, 'Christian Zionism in America: William E. Blackstone and the 1916 Petition' in *Jews and Messianism in the Modern Era: Metaphor and Meaning*, edited by Jonathan Frankel, Oxford University Press, 1991.

James Barr, *Fundamentalism*, 1977; 2nd edition, SCM Press, 1981.

W.E. Blackstone, *Jesus is Coming: A Scriptural Survey of the Arguments for a Literal, Personal and Pre-millennial Coming of the Lord and its Practical Character*, London, Pickering & Inglis, 2nd edition, 1928.

Leonardo Boff and Clodovis Boff, *Introducing Liberation Theology*, translated by Burns, Burns & Oates, 1987.

Madeleine Bunting, 'God's own bus service', *The Guardian Weekend*, 1 February 1997.

K. Burridge, *New Heaven, New Earth*, Blackwell, Oxford, 1971.

Billy Graham, *Approaching Hoofbeats: The Four Horsemen of the Apocalypse*, Hodder & Stoughton, 1984.

Vittorio Lanternari, *The Religions of the Oppressed*, New American Library, 1965.

Hal Lindsey, *The Late Great Planet Earth*, Lakeland, 1970.

Hal Lindsey, *The Rapture: Truth or Consequences*, Bantam Books, 1983.

John Mullin, Edward Luce and Clare Trevena, 'Fire from the Sun', *The Guardian*, 12 October 1994.

David Sexton, 'Books' column in *The Guardian*, 8 September 1995.

Shearer West, *Fin de Siècle: Art and Society in an Age of Uncertainty*, Bloomsbury, 1993.

Chapter 10

What Next?

'There won't be any more litter on the floor, or dirt. There won't be any more graffiti. The world will be a better place.'

Sarah Gibbons, aged 10

'Eventually the heat which the ozone layer is now unable to stop will cause the earth to heat up. The core of the earth will get so hot that it will explode and pieces of earth with gases surrounding them will fly off into space and all life forms will become extinct.'

Lara Thomas, aged 12

What, I wondered, do people with no preconceived ideas really think about the future and the end of the world. The answer seemed to be to ask children for their views, and these are two of their responses, which focus on the environment. Sarah is optimistic: if we can clean up a bit the world will be a better place. Indeed, many of her classmates added that it would be a happier place. Lara, on the other hand, sees the long-term consequences of pollution: it is too late to stop the process and, one way or another, this will be our undoing.

The last half of the twentieth century has developed two areas of knowledge which between them have revolutionized the way we perceive the world and how it might end: ecology and cosmology. In a sense they represent, in secular terms, the two divergent trends in religious thought that we have already encountered. Ecologists tend to offer us hope: if we look after the earth – and, increasingly, space – properly, we remain to some degree in control. If we choose to, we can halt the processes that could make the earth uninhabitable within a very short space of time, and this is Sarah's view too. Cosmologists, on the other hand, see that the end is beyond all human control, as young Lara senses, but here at least the timescale is so immense that it is barely conceivable. Either the universe will stop expanding and go into reverse, so ending in a 'big crunch' the evolution that began with the big bang; or else it will continue to expand, so that eventually all matter will decay into radiation.

And where, one might ask, is God in all this? The fundamentalist reaction is to cling to the hope that information about the end is encoded in the Bible, and there is no shortage of prophets ready to try their hand at decoding the message and putting to it a date in the fairly near future. Other Christians are more cautious, and are only now beginning to respond to the new sciences. One of the consequences of the environmental movement is that it has led the churches to reflect properly for the first time on human responsibility for God's creation. And, perhaps influenced in part by cosmological theory, there has come a similar growing awareness that, still living in the shadow of Augustine, the Christian church has not been very strong on eschatology. Archbishop Donald Coggan has reflected on the opening of Psalm 24, 'The earth is the Lord's', in these terms:

> If man, in his stupidity, were mad enough to blow this world to smithereens and to blot out all life upon it, that would not be the end. God, concerned as he is for his world, is not dependent on it for his continuing existence. He *is*. He will be – whatever happens on our little planet. We may ask whether this note is consistently heard from our pulpits. Are we weak on our eschatology? 'If it is for this life only that Christ has given us hope, we of all men are most to be pitied' (1 Corinthians 15:19). Are we affirming this? Or is our message so *this*-world centred that it has no *heavenly* content?

When my questions about the world and its end were put to three groups of schoolchildren aged between ten and thirteen, their answers reflected the twin secular preoccupations of environment and space that have characterized the 1990s.

Greening the end

On 5 March 1996 the ecologist Jonathon Porritt gave a lecture at the Royal Institution in London organized by the Religious Education and

Environment Programme, of which he is a patron. His aim was to try to persuade the world's religions to accept more direct responsibility for the ecological crisis, which he described as 'a crisis of the human spirit'. The religious response to date, according to Porritt, had been 'belated and very patchy'. He described Christians as 'very opposed, if not actually hostile to the ideas of creation spirituality, and what they see as paganism or flaky New Age mysticism', and he concluded that the church needed to 'reassess its teaching and contemporary witness on such issues'. The *Church Times* put a report of the lecture on its front page and gave it the headline: 'Faith only pale green, says Porritt'.

Elsewhere Porritt has lamented the dearth of philosophical debate within the Green movement. His argument is that thought needs to be given to the values that must replace those underlying two and a half centuries of industrialization responsible for the current crisis. Even so, he denies that ecologists fall into the same camp as religious millennialists:

> There is very little resemblance between the severe realism of the vast majority of mainstream environmentalists and the apocalyptic yearnings of the religious zealots and nutcases who would positively welcome the coming of an ecological or nuclear Armageddon as a prelude to the Second Coming of the Messiah. The fact that we humans have indeed usurped God's erstwhile role as the *potential* ender of time is an aspect of human nature and technological progress that cannot be denied.

While ecologists may not be actively seeking or welcoming the end of the world, they have not hesitated to use the language of religious apocalyptic to describe the possibility of it. Porritt describes global warming as a new topic supported by old fears – the end of the world by flooding. Similarly, changing agricultural patterns evoke the possibility of famines, while the rising incidence of skin cancers can be regarded as a modern pestilence.

Two things seem to have blocked a coherent Christian reaction to increasing environmental damage. One is the attitude which asks: where does the Bible talk about BSE or holes in the ozone or overpopulation? The answer is, nowhere, and so the fundamentalists' reaction is to do nothing; after all, they would argue, God is in control. Then, Christian belief in Christ's Second Coming at the end of the world can equally be interpreted as suggesting that there is no need to do anything; indeed, ecological decay, like the restoration of the Jews to Israel, might hurry the whole process up a bit. These attitudes have been condemned by Orthodox and Catholic theologians; belief in Christ's return is no excuse for inaction on the environment, they argue, and Cardinal Roger Etchegaray has spoken of humankind's 'pact of solidarity with creation'.

On the issue of the environment, at least, science and religion are in the main united in a certain reverence before nature. But in some Christian quarters there lurks a deep-rooted fear of appearing to worship the creation rather than the Creator, and where this is the case the environment loses out every time. The same cannot be said of the younger generation. If my correspondents are representative – and there is no reason to suppose that they are not – young adults in the early years of the twenty-first century will be more environmentally conscious than any generation before them.

In the responses of the younger age group there is a touching tendency to equate the end of pollution with greater human happiness. Ten-year-olds are keen on recycling, protecting the rain forests and saving endangered species, and furthermore (thanks, perhaps, to their teacher's prompting) they hate litter. Ten-year-old Heather writes that a world free from mess would be 'a lot healthier… This world would be a cleaner and friendlier world.' Even so, there is a certain urgency to some of their remedies: 'If people don't help, in a few years' time it will be too late,' says Kim, who calls for solar powered or electric cars. The children are also convinced that their contribution is important: 'WE MAKE THE DIFFERENCE,' concludes one, and 'we have made HISTORY,' says another, although several are a touch fatalistic: 'All we need to do is to keep it like this.' And an important ally for them is the micro-computer – presumably to help monitor all the mess.

Similar concerns emerged among a class of twelve- and thirteen-year-olds, and although their increased scientific knowledge enabled them to present a more detailed, and sometimes more frightening picture, many are still convinced that it is possible to do something about it. The hole in the ozone layer is mentioned repeatedly. Katherine Smith, aged twelve and three-quarters, puts it like this:

I think the end of the world would begin at Antarctica. The ozone layer hole would start stretching over the world. The atmosphere would disappear and dangerous ultra-violet rays would enter through the hole. Trees and plants would die, insects and animals would die, humans would die. The sky would become black with no stars or moon to light it. The sun would not appear but would send its harmful rays killing off everything. The heat would be so extreme that the remaining land would shrivel up. The water would evaporate leaving the world a small rock in the universe.

But Katherine also has a remedy to suggest: 'Before that astronauts would send all the people to Mars, giving each one protective clothing to withstand Mars' gravity.' The green generation is also the second space-age generation.

Outside causes

An asteroid will hurtle towards us and an alien life form will slowly position the earth and every living thing on it will be burned by the sun as it drifts through space towards it (Adam Lindop, aged 12).

'It's the end of the world,' shouts a character in the 1996 film *Independence Day*, as news arrives of a band of aliens advancing through the solar system like locusts, devouring all the natural resources of one planet before moving on to the next. Most of the fears that drove our ancestors to think in terms of the end of life on this earth have been contained. Today's aliens are yesterday's plagues and natural disasters, which used to engender the same terror: these things, it was thought, would bring about the end of human life on our planet and there was absolutely nothing anyone could do about it. And once medical science was able to protect humanity against virulent plague, once technology could begin to predict disasters and alleviate the destructive effects of most of them, people began to look further afield for signs of an end wholly outside human control.

The gap has been filled by modern cosmology. And it is intriguing that, far from allaying popular fears of alien invasions, an increased understanding of the universe has actually encouraged them. The aliens theory seems to acquire fresh momentum with each new discovery about conditions that might support some form of life somewhere in our solar system or way beyond it. An early example of a popular interpretation of astronomical observations was Percival Lowell's claim at the end of the nineteenth century that the lines visible on the surface of Mars were canals constructed by Martians to pipe water from the polar ice caps across the Martian deserts. As the Suez and Panama canals were under construction at the time, the lines seen by the astronomers were understood as the engineering achievements of an advanced civilization. The attraction of this theory for those caught up in *fin de siècle* excitement was irresistible.

Young Adam's view of the end combines aliens of science fiction and popular belief with a very real threat to the world from another body in the solar system. As we have already seen, objects that move across the sky, whether comets, meteors or asteroids, have always inspired fear and have been seen as signs of the end, even if it was not understood that they could in fact be the cause of the end. So far, of course, this has not happened, but with an average 200,000 tons of rock from space hitting the earth every year, some people would say that it is only a matter of time before a rock arrives that is big enough to inflict the ultimate destruction on our planet. The figures are not encouraging. According to Dr Duncan Steel of the Anglo-Australian Observatory, a 100-metre asteroid crashing through the atmosphere could devastate 10,000 square kilometres of land and kill 100,000 people; if it fell in the sea it could create a tidal wave that would kill a million people living in coastal areas. (Dr Steel suggests in his book that an event of such proportions happens every 1,000 years, although it is tempting to think that this figure owes at least something to popular mythology. Nonetheless, some astronomers are already predicting a devastating encounter between the earth and the remains of a giant comet at about the time of the next millennium – AD3000.) At the extreme, a massive collision, whether with an asteroid or a comet, on the same scale as the one which is now thought to have put an end to the dinosaurs 65 million years ago, would kill off all 6 billion of us and create a nuclear winter. So the floods, winds and the sun turning black, which might once have been dismissed as products of medieval writers' fevered imaginations, all take their place in the scientists' predictions.

Comets have a special place in the interaction between cosmology and eschatology. Their brightness, at least in an age without light pollution, has always made them striking portents – was the star of Bethlehem an appearance of Halley's Comet? – and nowadays the arrival of a new one tends to provoke fresh fears of a direct encounter. As debris from the big bang, propelled far out into space, comets have much to tell us about the origins of the universe, but not all the attention paid to them is particularly scientific. Sir Fred Hoyle once suggested that passing comets brought fresh waves of microbes (like influenza) to our planet, but fortunately, according to another theory of Hoyle's, our nostrils point downwards so that we are not as vulnerable to them as we might otherwise be.

Astronomy and apocalyptic were brought together very publicly in 1994 when the comet designated Shoemaker-Levy 9 was observed to be on a collision course with Jupiter. A Polish-born visionary, known by various names including Sofia Richmond and Sister Marie Gabriel, appeared in full-page advertisements in the British national press claiming that the collision would cause a fireball which would lead to global catastrophe unless humanity became obedient to the Ten Commandments and prayed to God for mercy. The collision duly took place, and between 16 and 22 July Jupiter was assailed by a stream of fragments of the comet. The following month Sister Marie Gabriel's prophecy appeared in a reworked form. Disaster had so far been averted by worldwide prayer, but her advertisements now proclaimed that a piece of the comet had strayed away from Jupiter and was heading for the earth, 'as a COSMIC SIGN from God to all nations to reduce the Crime Epidemic with draconian deterrents or face extinction'. There followed a series of demands, which ranged from ethical prescription (destroy all 'video nasties', abolish alcohol, ban guns) to animal rights (stop bull fighting, cruelty to birds, the ivory trade) to the purely personal (a demand that the German Government pay her compensation for the destruction of her family estate in Warsaw during World War II).

The collision between the comet and Jupiter received extensive media coverage, and Sister Marie Gabriel (who does not appear to be a member of any religious order) was able to take full advantage of the heightened public awareness of cosmic events. Her second prediction, though, fell flat. Not only was there no rogue fragment heading for earth, but she made the mistake of suggesting that Shoemaker-Levy 9 was really Halley's Comet, which was easily disproved by astronomers. But there will be other disintegrating comets and probably the world has not heard the last of this latest prophet of doom. After all, she has at her disposal not only the power of the world's press, but also huge amounts of astronomical data, which would have been beyond the wildest imaginings of prophets and visionaries of even the comparatively recent past.

The beginning and the end

Perhaps the most important contribution of cosmology to the end of the world debate has been the volume of research dedicated to the origins of the universe, focusing in particular on what happened in the first few minutes after the big bang. As knowledge of origins develops, so cosmologists can formulate increasingly sophisticated hypotheses as to how it will all end. Paul Davies is probably the best-known cosmologist working in this field, thanks to his award-winning books written in language that those with a non-scientific background can understand.

The problem with cosmology is that it deals in expanses of time which, as Davies himself admits, can defy human imagination. The current age of the universe is put at roughly 15,000 million years, although estimates can vary by a few thousand million. It is a figure arrived at by measuring the rate at which the universe is expanding, although recent observations from the Hubble space telescope have suggested that it does not expand at a constant rate – hence the discrepancies. However, since some stars, including some in our own galaxy, are at least 14,000 million years old, the figure seems close enough, at least to a non-scientist.

But this vast reach of time is nothing compared with what is still to come. As far as our immediate future is concerned, our sun is about halfway through its estimated lifespan of 10,000 million years. Davies suggests that the earth could remain habitable for another 2,000 to 3,000 million years (and human beings have only existed for a mere 5 million years), although he surrounds this with caveats: problems of energy supply and population control will need to be sorted, and damage to the environment and from the impact of asteroids will have to be limited. By then, if human beings survive, there is every reason to suppose that they will have the technology to leave the earth before the sun burns out and seek refuge elsewhere in the universe. As for the universe itself, cosmologists are still undecided as to whether it will collapse in on itself or continue to expand for ever, although an answer to the problem is reckoned to be not many years away. In his book *The Last Three Minutes*, Paul Davies outlines what might happen in each case, and this is where the numbers really get out of hand.

In the case of infinite expansion, Davies imagines the scenario in a trillion trillion years' time, when the universe will be 10,000 million times its present size. While the expanding universe tries to pull objects further apart, mutual gravitational attraction will try to bring them together. The result is burnt out stars coalescing in spinning black holes, which will eventually disappear. Physical processes come to an end: it is a state of 'eternal death'. But it is hardly going to happen overnight.

The same is true if the universe ceases to expand and begins to contract towards a big crunch. Davies verges on the poetic:

The universe would slowly transform itself into an all-encompassing cosmic furnace, grilling all fragile life-forms wherever they might be hiding, and stripping away planetary atmospheres.

As the universe approaches its final phase it would return to the conditions that obtained at the moment of its creation. 'Which is worse?' asks Davies. 'A universe slowly degenerating and expanding forever toward a state of dark emptiness or one that implodes to fiery oblivion?'

I count myself among those who are completely gripped by such questions, despite my feeble understanding of them. Yet for many people such talk of beginnings and endings is too remote to have any relevance. Religious leaders seem to be divided. Rabbi Lionel Blue, interviewed after some of the findings of the Hubble telescope were published in February 1996, declared, 'I'm fascinated but it's not really relevant… a pleasant diversion.' A Muslim leader, Akbar Ahmed, saw in it a justification of the statement in the Koran that God made universes, plural. While the Roman Catholic Bishop of Leeds, David Konstant, argued that the theological understanding of the beginning of the universe as being an act of creation 'from nothing' means that the question of how it all began is one that science cannot answer. So where *is* God in all this?

Where is God?

Paul Davies dates the idea that the universe is dying from 1856, when the German physicist Hermann von Helmholtz predicted its 'heat death'. This, says Davies, was used to support 'a philosophy of atheism, nihilism and despair'. This depression lasted a long time. In 1923 the philosopher Bertrand Russell wrote:

> All the labours of the ages, all the devotion, all the inspiration, all the noonday brightness of human genius, are destined to extinction in the vast death of the solar system; and the whole temple of Man's achievement must inevitably be buried beneath the debris of a universe in ruins.

The desire to try to make sense of the universe has been implicit in all the ideas about the end of time we have encountered in the course of this book.

For Russell, the atheist philosopher, the thought that the universe was dying was a source of despair. Since then, humankind's knowledge about the nature and history of the universe has advanced beyond all recognition, and many scientists are much more inclined to stand in awe of it. Paul Davies' conclusion is certainly more circumspect than Russell's:

> If there is a purpose to the universe, and it achieves that purpose, then the universe must end, for its continued existence would be gratuitous and pointless. Conversely, if the universe endures forever, it is hard to imagine that there is any ultimate purpose to the universe at all. So cosmic death may be the price that has to be paid for cosmic success. Perhaps the most that we can hope for is that the purpose of the universe becomes known to our descendants before the end of the last few minutes.

For a Christian perspective on all this I went to listen to a lecture by Professor John Polkinghorne, who is both a physicist and a priest and theologian in the Church of England. Perhaps predictably, one of his main arguments was that the question of the scientist – how did the universe come into being? – and that of the theologian – why did it? – are not incompatible and both need to be answered. Explaining how the universe came about does not prevent us from saying that it is the will of God that holds it in being and sustains it. Professor Polkinghorne pointed frequently to the complexity of the universe which enables human life to exist. Life needs a steady, long-lived source of energy, and so we have a sun which burns for millions of years; the universe needs to last long enough for life to evolve – 10,000 million years or so just for the basic raw materials of life to be assembled. If a detail such as the force of gravity were changed only slightly, the universe would be sterile. It is a picture of a finely tuned world – a universe in a trillion – which demands some kind of explanation.

As a theologian Polkinghorne has no doubt that human beings have a destiny beyond death. He argued that since the 'pattern that is me' is dissolved in death, God will recreate that pattern in a new environment of his choosing – a new creation. And his overall view was of God interacting with the world rather than intervening in it.

Since he had spoken on the origins of the universe I asked somewhat tentatively about the end of it. The scientist's answer was that of course the universe was bound to die, although on a time scale of tens of billions of years. The theologian's answer also drew on our perception of time. We were reminded of the Christian assumption, held until relatively recently, that the universe was not very old and that it would not be long before Christ returned to wind up the whole operation. Now we know otherwise. God is not in a hurry. It took many millions of years for the human race to emerge, yet the universe was even then still in its infancy, so despite what the Christmas hymn would have us believe, Jesus did not in fact come 'late in time'. Speaking as a theologian, John Polkinghorne's conclusion was that Jesus' Second Coming would be as strange and as unexpected as his first. As he wrote some years ago:

> It seems that it is God's way to work slowly and almost secretly. When we think of all those thousands of millions of years which elapsed from the big bang till the universe saw the emergence of life, we see that he is not a God in a hurry. He is a God of process and not of magic. Perhaps there is no other way for love to work if it is to respect the integrity of the beloved.

Why the end?

Exactly why people have expected the world to end when they have is a question which has exercised anthropologists, psychologists and social scientists to quite a degree. There seems to be no reason, say, why one race oppressed by foreign rulers should seek refuge in end-of-the-world beliefs, while another in identical circumstances does not. However, according to Burridge, whom I have already quoted several times, one theme common to various millennial movements is the hope of moral regeneration, and the possibility of creating new and better communities.

This idea of regeneration is certainly there in the minds of the schoolchildren who sent me their essays on the end. While many did just as they were asked and described, often very graphically, what they thought would happen at the end, others reflected on why the end would come at all. They almost all agreed that it would be our fault: 'All humans will eventually turn against each other, for reasons of greed, power, money. This would cause wars,' wrote thirteen-year-old Joanne, who had already described the catastrophic effects of global warming. Carlie blamed computers: the next generation of children will be taught at home and 'won't be as clever as our generation because we are taught naturally by human beings who have learnt many things because they have really lived'.

If everything is getting worse, is there anything we can do about it? The younger children were unanimous that not only can we halt the process of environmental destruction but that we will be better and happier people as a result. This was as close as they came to a golden age of regeneration, though twelve-year-old David Murphy had a novel suggestion: on-going regeneration thanks to friendly aliens, who would come to 'make the earth a cleaner place without any industry and they would come back if the pollution got too high again'.

Burridge has a different conclusion: 'The millennium points to a condition of being in which humans become free-movers, in which there are no obligations, in which all earthly desires are satisfied, and therefore expunged. A new earth merges into the new heaven.' Certainly this is an explanation which seems valid for movements such as the Hau-haus in New Zealand. But it is a brave soul who tries to formulate something which will cover all kinds of end-of-the-world movements and still be useful. Christians, for example, would certainly take issue with the ideal of being 'free-movers', since the Christian view of both this world and the next is one of service and worship. But perhaps here too the lack of a suitable global definition proves my point: human thinking and belief about the end is too varied, and gloriously so, to be so narrowly contained.

Journey's end

When I began to plan my investigation into the end of time, one of the first anecdotes I came across concerned a nineteenth-century Doctor of Divinity, one William Ramsey. In 1857 Dr Ramsey wrote to a friend who was studying biblical prophecies on the end of the world and advised him to stop his research: 'I never knew a man who began to study them and to write on them who did not ultimately go crazy,' he wrote, even though he himself had written a treatise entitled 'On the Second Coming of the Lord before the Millennium.' I hope I have not yet given anyone cause for concern as far as my sanity goes, although some of the latter-day prophets I have encountered certainly fall into the category of the more than slightly dotty.

At the end of this book I am increasingly aware of the number of different paths my research might have taken, and indeed may yet follow. My starting point was to assume that people at all times and in all kinds of places have been regularly caught up in thinking about how the world – or at least their bit of it – might end. What I had not bargained for, though, was the sheer number of different contexts, both sacred and secular, but particularly secular, in which these ideas would pop up throughout recorded history. Another person adopting a similar approach would probably come up with a totally different set of investigations. It all depends where you are, what religious tradition you come from, what you read and even what pictures or films you look at.

As a Christian I have been surprised at the extent to which the basic Christian imagery of the end-times is ingrained in human consciousness. I have also been disturbed by some of the extreme doctrines on the end which purport to have their basis in Christian scripture. The way in which some Christians actively promote the restoration of the Jews to Israel because they think in so doing they can achieve their own salvation is both theologically unsound and morally objectionable. When a certain brand of Protestantism capitalizes on the misfortunes of a whole race in order to further its own interests, there must be something deeply flawed in its interpretation of biblical texts.

Representations of the end of time are far from being all doom and gloom. Christians will not be surprised at this; nor, indeed, will anyone who has ever attended a Christian funeral service and heard read the wonderful vision of a new heaven and a new earth from Revelation 21 – the promise that there God will dwell with his people: 'He will wipe away every tear from their eyes, and death shall be no more, neither shall there be mourning nor crying nor pain any more, for the former things have passed away.' It is an optimistic view of the future which has its secular echoes in the romantic legends of returning heroes and finds artistic expression in some of the painting of the Pre-Raphaelites.

The idea that human beings may be at least to some extent in control of their own destiny is equally pervasive, from the first Zoroastrians through to today's environmentalists. But although care for the created order has to become an urgent Christian priority, it has never been part of orthodox Christian belief that humankind has any influence as to when the end may come. God will bring the present age to an end in his time, not ours. And whether the date on the calendar is the year 2000 or 20000 has, I believe, nothing to do with it. But that will not stop people speculating about numbers and dates, and probably it is healthy that they should continue to do so. If ever we cease to wonder how and when it will all end, then surely something will have gone badly wrong with our natural curiosity and imagination.

T.S. Eliot wrote in *Little Gidding* that 'to make an end is to make a beginning'.

I should like to think that the end of my journey will mark the beginning of many others, undertaken by people who share my fascination with this many-faceted subject of the end of time.

References

K. Burridge, *New Heaven, New Earth*, Oxford, Blackwell, 1971.

Donald Coggan, *A New Day for Preaching*, SPCK, 1996.

Paul Davies, *The Last Three Minutes: Conjectures about the Ultimate Fate of the Universe*, Weidenfeld and Nicolson, London, 1994.

John Polkinghorne, *The Way the World Is: The Christian Perspective of a Scientist*, Triangle Books, 1983.

Jonathon Porritt, Foreword to Martin Palmer, *Dancing to Armageddon*, The Aquarian Press, London, 1992.

George Smoot and Keay Davidson, *Wrinkles in Time: The Imprint of Creation*, Little, Brown & Co., 1993.

ACKNOWLEDGMENTS

Samuel Beckett, *Endgame*, 1958, page 35. Used by permission of Faber and Faber, 1967, and Grove/Atlantic Inc. (NY).

Robert Heilbroner, *Visions of the Future: The Distant Past, Yesterday, Today and Tomorrow*. Copyright © 1995 Robert Heilbroner. Used by permission of Oxford University Press (NY).

Abba Hillel Silver, *Where Judaism Differs*, 1956; London, Collier Macmillan (NY), 1989. Used by permission of Collier Macmillan.

Tom Stoppard, *Rosencrantz and Guildenstern are Dead*, Act 2, page 52. Used by permission of Faber and Faber, 1967, and Grove/Atlantic Inc. (NY).

Gerd Theissen, *The Shadow of the Galilean: The Quest of the Historical Jesus in Narrative Form*, translated by John Bowden, SCM Press (London), 1987. Used by permission of SCM Press and Augsburg Fortress (USA).